John Fisher was a man with a calling to  about our dogs. This he did, all over the v insights into dog behaviour and his huge, h while sharing his knowledge on stage anc This, his fourth book, enables everyone in v.... w.... dogs to touch once more that rare combination of talents from a very special friend and pioneering thinker

Peter Neville, Centre of Applied Pet Ethology

Dedication

To John, who may not be with us, but can still make us laugh.
Very few people touch our lives and leave such a gift

Diary of a 'dotty dog' Doctor.

John Fisher

Edited by Sarah Whitehead

Cartoons by Russell Jones

First published in 1998 by Alpha Publishing
75 St. Andrew Crescent,
Windsor, Berkshire SL4 4EP.

ISBN–0–9532814–0–X

Printed in Great Britain by
Bookham Print and Design

Cover photograph courtesy of Dave King.

For further details of books, videos and products please send a stamped addressed envelope
to: Greengarth, Maddox Lane, Bookham, Surrey KT23 3HT.

John Fisher's course, 'Understanding the Canine/Human Interface' is available through
The Animal Care College, Ascot House, High Street, Ascot, Berkshire, SL5 7JG.
Telephone: 01344 28269 for a full syllabus.

CONTENTS

FOREWORD:

My wife, Liz, keeps horses and as all horse people know, they are not cheap to keep. People often ask me if I ride and I tell them that I don't, I just seem to pay the bills. It came as no surprise, but I thought a little pointed, when Liz called her new horse Bilbao and nicknamed him Bill. Our farrier is also called Bill and now, when Bill comes to shoe Bill, he brings me a bill. Sometimes, I feel like a pelican - no matter which way I look, there's an enormous great bill in front of me.

The point of this story is to introduce our farrier, Bill Harrison, because it is on his suggestion, almost insistence, that this book has been written. Bill has read all of my previous books and he has always commented how much he has enjoyed the occasional case history that I have written about. Five years ago, he suggested that I put them all together into a 'James Herriot-style' book of cases, some serious and some a bit oddball - as he said, I must have hundreds of them by now. On almost every visit since then, he has asked me if I have written THAT book yet and the answer is now - YES!

This book is therefore written for Bill Harrison and I hope he enjoys it. I also hope that he considers the number of hours it has taken for me to complete it just to please him. I further hope that the next time Bill comes to shoe Bill, the bill he brings is not as big as the bill he usually brings - is that OK with you Bill?

JOHN FISHER

INTRODUCTION
John Rogerson

It takes a great deal of courage, commitment and belief in what you are doing to be one of the first in a new and unproved field. Jonn Fisher was one of the first real 'dog people' to get involved in behaviour therapy and lead the way for many others to follow.

My own friendship with John goes back over 20 years when we were fellow competitors in the sport of working trials. I competed with a working sheepdog and John a long-coated German Shepherd. We both qualified our dogs to be working trials champions at around the same time and also went on to judge one another in competitions. Competitors would get together after the working part of the day and many were the nights we would swap stories in the local pub. John often led the jokes and seemed to have an endless supply of humorous tales to tell, almost all of which were based on real-life situations. We then lost touch with one another for a while as we both got heavily involved in the more serious aspects of trying to make a living in a totally untried occupation - dog behaviour consultant and training advisor. Compared to training dogs to compete in working trials, this was very serious stuff. Owners would be paying for advice on everything from curing aggression to stopping their dog from barking. Paying clients would generally not tolerate failure and the consequences of giving inappropriate advice could result in injury to the clients or the destruction of the dog. No place for humour here you would concede. But every so often a client would either have a problem that seemed so bizarre or come out with a statement that was so funny that you would not be human if you did not either laugh inwardly, or more embarrassingly, burst out laughing in front of the puzzled owners.

John was one of the best in the world at not only sorting out behaviour problems but also at capturing and then relating the more humorous incidents that took place within the confines of his consulting room in a converted stable, attached to his home in Surrey. I have lost count of the number of 'client' stories he was able to tell when we resumed contact through our professional interests, but I can tell you that his stories outnumbered mine by a ratio of ten to one! It's not that I don't get wacky clients, bizarre behaviour problems or funny remarks, it's just that John was a master of remembering every incident and then relating them in his own witty, inimitable way.

I remember having a social get-together with John and a few other dog friends when we all told our most embarrassing stories. I started out: my wife Moira, who runs a busy dog grooming business from our home, had booked in a client for six o'clock, but had not written in what problem the clients were having with their dog. When the appointed hour arrived I was ready and waiting, having just seen the penultimate client of the day. Six-fifteen arrived and still no clients. Six-thirty, six-fifty, obviously they were not going to make the appointment and did not have the decency to phone and cancel, so I settled down to relax for the evening. Five minutes later there was a knock on the front door and two elderly people stood looking apologetic, with their Irish Setter in tow. They apologised profusely for being late but explained that they had been held up in traffic and had encountered some difficulty in finding the house. Slightly peeved, I invited them in and sat them down in my consulting room. I then hurriedly started asking them questions about their dog's behaviour. What time do you feed him? What toys does he play with? Where does he sleep at night? What is he like with visitors that come to your house? The questions continued unabated for around ten minutes and I then asked the increasingly uncomfortable-looking owners to describe any problems that they were having with their dog, Red. They looked at one another and then the gentleman replied that

Red was not good at returning when he was called. He would often run up to other dogs when out for exercise and took a great deal of catching. This was obviously just a simple training problem as no aggression was involved, so I immediately described how to divide all the dog's food up into portions and use these portions to teach a good recall. I also described the use of a long line attached to the dog's collar and gave them a demonstration of how to do this in my consulting room. We then took the dog outside and worked for 20 minutes on teaching the dog how to come when called. The owners were not enthusiastic enough when the dog returned, so 1 made them get really excited and jump up and down when the dog responded correctly. We then went back into the house where I began writing their recall programme down so that they would remember what to do at home. Eventually, I was interrupted by an embarrassed owner who said that he felt there was some misunderstanding. His daughter had made the appointment and had booked the dog in for bathing and grooming! Quick as a flash, I ran to find Moira and asked if she was expecting a dog. Yes, she replied it was a new customer with a dog for bathing and grooming at 6.30 but they had not turned up and neither had they bothered to phone!

When John's turn came he captivated everyone with his tales of mistaken identity, misinterpretation, and just plain stupidity on the part of the clients; some simply too outrageous to relate in a book!

What John has left us with is the ability to look at life and all the problems that it throws at us and still maintain the ability to smile. The ability to make other people smile is very rare indeed - John had an abundant supply of this most precious gift. Read and enjoy.

DEAR DIARY

Dateline: September 1996
I have just sat down to write this book and from now until I have finished it, I will be seeing very few cases myself. My practice will continue to run under the guidance of my head of practice, Sarah Whitehead, at our HQ in Surrey and through my associate counsellors at various veterinary establishments in London and the Home Counties. The case histories recorded in this book are therefore all cases seen before this date and some stretch back many years. However, they are all true records of events, even if some of them seem a little incredulous and make you wonder, do people really treat their pets like this? The answer to that question is, yes, some people do - not many I admit, but enough to make writing a book like this worthwhile and, I hope, amusing to read. Perhaps I should explain.

I run a busy pet behaviour counselling practice, which accepts referrals only from veterinary surgeons. The majority of our case-load involves problem dogs or cats, but I personally tend to specialise in dog problems. We occasionally treat the odd feather-plucking parrot, or over-sexed tortoise and if you have a rabbit with a phantom pregnancy, then we can deal with that, too. Because we work strictly on referral, this gives clients the impression that I am a doctor, hence the title of the book. I am not. In fact, I have no higher academic qualifications at all, unless you count 'O' level woodwork. I qualify to do the job through years of practical experience of working with dogs and studying the subject of animal behaviour since its increase in popularity in the UK over the last ten years, or so. I have written three serious books on the subject and edited another and I lecture to veterinary audiences and other interested groups internationally. Other counsellors in my practice hold various degrees, diplomas and certificates in the subject, but it seems silly for me to try and obtain one, as I am usually asked to tutor some part of their qualifying course. In 1989, I was commissioned to write and tutor a correspondence course for the Animal Care College called, 'Understanding the Canine/Human Interface', which has since enrolled over 1000 students world-wide. So, as you can see, my main field of activity now concentrates on educating others in this very important subject, but that doesn't mean the subject is always very serious. Sometimes it has its lighter moments and that's exactly what this book is all about.

We are constantly hearing reports about how good pets are for people. Scientific studies have shown that pet owners are generally healthier and more relaxed than non pet owners and that stroking your pet can have a calming effect on your heart and pulse rate. I don't entirely agree with this. For sure, I don't doubt that the majority of pets are good for the majority of owners, but the pet owners I see are usually bordering on a nervous breakdown as a direct result of owning the pet they are presenting for treatment. These pets are definitely not good for their owners and part of our job as counsellors is not only to improve the behaviour of the animal, but also to try and rebuild the relationship which has inevitably broken down between them and their people. In over 50 per cent of the cases we see, the owners report that we are the last resort before considering having the animal euthanased. As with any form of counselling, it can be quite stressful to be constantly soaking up other people's fears, anxieties and often their frustration and anger. I make these comments to highlight the professional responsibilities of the job that we do: the light-hearted approach to it which follows is in no way meant to devalue these responsibilities. The names of most of the people and their pets have been changed to protect the guilty and those that I have managed to contact have been only too pleased to have their case history anonymously reported. Some, I have lost touch with and if you recognise yourself within these pages, I want to assure you that your case was approached as seriously as any other, it's just that in hindsight, there were amusing aspects to it which warrant its inclusion in 'Dotty Dogs'.

As a fairly new profession, which is still struggling for recognition in some areas of the veterinary world, it might be said that this is not a good time to 'send it up'. Established professions, like medical doctors, have been humorously portrayed for years, with films like 'Carry On Doctor' as a classic example. Even the dangerously invasive work of surgeons has been comically portrayed in television programmes like 'Surgical Spirit'. The question might well be asked, when is the best time to portray a serious profession in an amusing light? The answer is easy - before someone else does!

IT'S A TOUGH LIFE!

or

THE HILLS ARE ALIVE WITH THE SOUND OF BULL***T

Dateline: March 1996

As I have stated, my background is a practical one. I started my career as a prison dog handler following completion of an initial course at Durham police headquarters. Although I no longer train dogs, it is always a refreshing change from counselling people with problem pets to 'go back to basics' whenever I get the chance. An opportunity to do just that arose when I got a call from a man who lives in the Swiss Alps, asking if I would go and teach his Labrador to jump into water. Well, how could I resist, especially when he added that the cost of such a visit would be no problem! First of all, I checked to make sure I heard him right.

"You did say Labrador?"

"Yes."

"You did say jump into the water?"

"Yes."

"You did say the Swiss Alps?"

"Yes."

"I'll be on the next plane!"

As I stood on the shore of a beautiful lake in Luzern, gazing up at the incredible mountain that's on all the Swiss chocolate boxes, I thought to myself, all I said was THINK DOG (my first book) and look where it got me. Turning to my host who was stood holding two of the most well-balanced Labradors you have ever met, a black Lab called Andy, and a yellow Lab called Fergie, I said, "So Andy won't jump in the water. Does he know he's a Labrador?"

"Oh, yes," said my host. "He jumped in the day after I called you, and he loves it now."

"So, why am I here?" I asked in a worried tone, thinking that my four-day trip to the Alps was about to be cut short.

"Fergie's got a gundog test on Sunday and I would like you to help me train her for it, if you don't mind," he added.

Knowing that what I knew about gundog training could be written on a bullet, I confidently replied, "Of course I'll help."

Over a leisurely lunch, he explained what the test was all about. First, there would be a conformation and movement test, then someone would fire a gun whilst someone else threw a dummy, which the dog would have to pick up. This would be followed by four dogs being let off the lead together to see if they were sociable and then they would be expected to walk with their owner through a group of noisy people. Next, they would have to walk down a woodland path where some more dummies had been thrown into the woods, and the dog would be expected to indicate one of them without being given a command. Finally, they would go for a swim. I suggested that if he got Fergie out of the garden pond, where she had been practising the final part of the test for the last five minutes, we could take her out and run through some of the exercises.

Later that afternoon, I was stood in an Alpine pasture under a brilliant blue sky, the scenery shrouded in a misty haze. In one hand I had a starting pistol, in the other I had a dummy. Drawing on all my years of dog training experience, I fired the gun and threw the dummy. Fergie ran and picked it up. As I marvelled at how well I had just trained her, the haze cleared and I was surrounded by the most incredible mountain scenery. I swear I heard Julie Andrews and a group of nuns singing.

"That was good," said my host. "What shall we do now?"

"I'll go and hide some dummies in those trees over there and we'll see if she indicates one of them," I said. I hid four and Fergie brought all four back without being told and without having seen me hide them - then the nuns sang again.

"Do you think it would be a good idea to take Fergie into Luzern so that she gets used to noisy people," said my host.

"That's exactly what I was going to suggest," I said, and then told him that he was obviously a natural dog trainer to have thought of that himself - besides, I wanted to see Luzern.

We spent two pleasant hours seeing the sights. Fergie watched the street musicians, made friends with all the people she met, travelled in lifts, visited cafes, watched the swans and the ducks and walked in and out of traffic, children and prams. Absolutely nothing phased her. I was beginning to realise that I was in fact a very gifted gundog trainer.

That evening, we were invited to dinner at the home of my host's veterinary surgeons and I was pleasantly surprised to discover that I knew them. They had been on a course where I was lecturing in Germany the previous year and so we had a lot in common. My host told them of the work we had done that day and how well Fergie was being trained by me. It's not polite to contradict someone else's statement, so I didn't. After dinner, I was taken back to my very sumptuous hotel suite, where I had a night-cap on the balcony overlooking the lake and the mountains, before switching off my alarm clock and retiring to bed. My host was not picking me up until 10.30am and I remember falling asleep thinking, it's all go this dog training lark.

We had a full day's training in front of us before the big test on Sunday and as we walked the dogs through the woods at the edge of the lake, the following day I suggested we should do some work.

"You take the dogs out of sight," I said. "I'll go over there and hide some more dummies."

I hid four and Fergie retrieved four, so we went to see the statue of Christ that overlooks the lake, then we visited some vineyards, then we looked at the castle and then the chapel and then realised it was lunch time. The afternoon followed a similar pattern, except we didn't hide any dummies. Following a wonderful meal in a lovely restaurant, we retired for an early night.

I was picked up at 11.00 the next morning and we drove to the venue in the mountains. Over 60 gundogs were entered for the test and Fergie was not due to take it until 2.30 - so we went for another lunch at another lovely mountain restaurant. At 2.30 Fergie stood for the judge's examination and as soon as the judge touched her, she keeled over on her back to have her tummy tickled. Next, she retrieved the shot dummy, played with four other dogs, wagged her tail at the noisy crowd, retrieved the dummies from the woods (the only dog to get them all) and then went for a swim. She ended up with the highest marks and my host could not praise me enough for all the work I had done. Now that both Andy and Fergie have passed their tests, they can be mated and the pups will get their pedigree papers. At the moment, my host does not know whether the pups will be born in Luzern, his chalet higher up in the Alps, or on his 200-acre farm in the south of France. Whatever he decides, he wants me to go back and see them, which of course I have reluctantly agreed to do. You see, it's the pressure of all this work that is getting to me. To prove the point, within two days of returning from Switzerland, I had to pack again to go on a lecture tour of America, as well as visiting Disneyland, Beverly Hills, N.A.S.A. - you name it, I had to do it. It's a tough life working with dogs.

Comment:

My host had been a very successful business man, but was now retired. During his career, he was used to winning and now that his hobby was his dogs, he wanted to be successful in that field, too. He had done a very good job with both dogs, not only with their sociability, but also with their general level of control. I suppose I was invited to act as a sort of crutch and to give his confidence a boost. Perhaps he thought I might be able to see an area where I could improve Fergie's performance, but as it happened, I was there as a spectator making dog training noises.

Whatever the reason, he could afford to have (what he considered to be) the best and because he had read one of my books, he obviously thought I knew what I was talking about. It just goes to show that you can fool some of the people, some of the time.... but providing the majority of those which can be fooled live in the rich zone, I don't mind at all.

Regardless of why I was there, both my host and his wife were wonderfully hospitable and the dogs were delightful to work and play with. What came through loud and clear during my visit was how very proud he was of both dogs. If Fergie had not done very well at the test, he would have blamed himself and not the dog. This is a refreshing attitude that we see a lot of in the pet/owner relationship. The next case highlights this sense of pride.

IT'S A WOLF!

Dateline: August 1990

The phone call stated that they didn't really have a problem with their dog, they just wanted to make sure that they were doing the right things. Yes, they had been referred by their vet and no, they wouldn't see anybody else at the practice, it had to be John Fisher.

At the appointed time, my clients' estate car pulled up in our car park and a very big man climbed out of the driver's side. Well, at first sight I thought it was a man, but then I wasn't too sure, so I just said good morning - hedging my bets a bit. He, or she, helped a lady out of the passenger side who was clearly disabled. From the back seat climbed a young lady with a baby in her arms and she helped out a toddler who was about 18 months old. They all congregated around the tail gate, while the big man/woman frantically tried to attach a lead to an animal that was desperately trying to jump out. After a struggle, it was finally captured and out jumped a ten-month-old wolf crossed with a Siberian Husky. Now, I don't hold with wolf hybrids of any sort, but if you're going to cross a wolf with anything, don't use a breed as wolf-like as the Siberian - use a Basset Hound, or a Chihuahua - especially as it later turned out that these were first-time pet owners

Finally, once we got settled in my office and all the coffee cups had been placed above head-height, way out of tail-swiping range of the clumsy oaf which was bouncing around the room like an electric frog, I was able to get more information. His name was Remus - well, it would be, wouldn't it? It was clear to me that the owners looked upon him as a pure wolf and were very proud of him. He was a very striking animal, rangy like a wolf but with all the markings of the Siberian. He was also a very friendly animal, but his frequent and very exaggerated play bows towards me concerned me a little. A play bow in a dog is an invitation to play, but the posture is such that they can escape quickly if the invitation is rejected. There are therefore elements of conflict involved and the last thing I wanted was to be trapped in my office with a part wolf in a state of conflict. I told the owners that I was going to ignore Remus for a while, to give him time to realise I was not a threat and to give him a chance to relax a bit. Hopefully, this would stop him from using the chairs as a springboard to bounce himself off the walls. By this time, they had been in my office for 15 minutes. We hadn't even started the consultation and I still had no idea why they had come to see me.

The disabled lady was the owner and I asked her how she thought I could help her with Remus. She had read a lot of books about wolves and she just wanted to know whether I thought that Remus was happy living with them! That was it; that was the purpose of her visit. Before I could answer - not that I knew how to answer - the younger lady (her daughter), asked if I thought that the wolf would ever attempt to rip her children's throats out. I was becoming slightly dazed by now, when suddenly the big man/woman stated that I couldn't possibly answer these questions until I knew everything. Oh no, I thought! There's more.

Apparently, the big man/woman, was in fact a man - but only temporarily. He was the owner's son and his name was Carol. He used to be a policeman, but now he was a registered carer for his mother and was also undergoing a sex change. What he wanted to know was whether the hormone treatment he/she was on was affecting Remus's behaviour. Remus answered this question for me by suddenly launching himself at 'Carol the copper', wrapping his front legs around his arm and making highly suggestive thrusting movements. At this point, my dazed state turned to one of total shock. Then, I had a glimmer of hope. I know, I thought. I'm on candid camera - what a good wheeze. WRONG - these people were for real and they were expecting my mouth to start working any minute.

I can only assume that it did work, because the next time I looked at the clock they had been with me for nearly two hours, but for the life of me I can't remember what was said. I do know that every time I started to get a grasp of the situation, they would drop another bombshell:

"You can tell he's a wolf in lots of different ways," said Carol.

"Give me an example," I stupidly asked.

"Well, you know when wolves get ready to go hunting - they howl don't they?"

"Yes," I replied.

"Well, Remus does that when we pick his lead up."

"Oh! really," I said. "What do you do about it?"

"Nothing," said Carol. "We join in."

Can you imagine living next door to these people? Remus was walked four times a day and the neighbours were obviously exposed to this group howl every time. You can imagine the comments - "Hark Ethel, they're taking that dog out again."

To this day, I still don't know the reason for their visit, but I received frequent calls from them over the course of the next weeks, including one in which Carol reported that Remus had become aggressive. I asked what had happened and was told that he had started barking furiously at an air vent in the kitchen during the evening. I suggested that he could hear people outside and that they should shut the kitchen door. Apparently, this was not possible as it was an open-plan house. I suggested that they should cover the air vent in some way, but was told that they had tried that with a towel, but

Remus had jumped up and ripped it off. I muttered something about normal territorial behaviour and trying not to respond so that his barking was not rewarded - or some such thing - and managed to get off the phone. The following morning, I got another call.

"We've solved the problem," said Carol.

"What, you've stopped him barking?" I asked, eager to hear about a new technique which works on an almost insurmountable problem.

"No, we haven't stopped him, but we know why he's doing it. Mother reads tarot cards and apparently it has upset some born-again Christians who are holding prayer meetings for her salvation in the road outside the house."

"Well, there you go."

This was the only thing I could think of to say.

Comment:

Without doubt the dog has descended from the wolf. DNA profiles of all domestic dogs have been compared and found to be so alike that there is little doubt they have a common ancestry. These profiles almost exactly match the wolf and we know that the two species can interbreed. However, the domestic dog has been selectively bred over many centuries for its lack of reactivity. The wolf, on the other hand is a highly efficient predator, whose behaviour is 'hard wired' once it reaches sexual maturity. For sure, we can socialise wolves from a very young age so that they lose their fear of man, but just like any other wild animal, once they become adult, they will revert to a wild lifestyle. It only needs a sudden scream, or a child to have a temper tantrum to switch on their predatory instincts and if this happens, they cannot stop themselves - it's innate behaviour. With the current pressures being placed on dogs by the various anti-dog brigades and the draconian measures laid down in the infamous Dangerous Dogs Act, the last thing we need to do is to introduce pure wolf blood back into the dog. Anyone breeding wolf hybrids and selling them on as pets is being totally irresponsible and obviously has no real love for the wolf as the magnificent animal it is. More importantly, they can never claim to be dog lovers, or they would not risk adding to the pressure already exerted on the dog.

IN DENIAL

Dateline: April 1995

It's not just the people I meet who leave me open-mouthed, some people can do it by phone. I received a call from a lady who told me that her vet had suggested she ring me, to see whether I could give her any advice about a chewing problem that she had with her English Bull Terrier. For some reason, I immediately assumed that we were talking about a puppy and told her that it was normal developmental and experimental behaviour, much like human babies put thing in their mouths.

"Oh! No," she said. "He's not a puppy, he's 18 months old. In fact, he was very good as a puppy, he hardly chewed anything up."

Ah ha, I thought! We're probably talking about a separation anxiety, usually exhibited by dogs who are over-attached to their owners and become very distraught when they are left at home alone.

"Is he very attached to you?" I asked.

"Well yes, I suppose he is," she replied.

"Does he follow you from room to room and even try to get into the loo with you?"

"I suppose he does a bit, he likes to know where we are and what we're doing."

"Does he only chew when you are not there?" I said, certain that I had diagnosed the problem.

"No. It's when we're with him," she said. I detected a hint of 'that's a stupid question' in her voice.

Got it, I thought! It's attention-seeking behaviour. Some dogs are like children - they don't really mind whether attention is good or bad. Being told off for chewing, or being chased around the house by the owner trying to rescue something from their mouths, is better than being ignored. It reminds me of the searching question that Scottish comedian Billy Connolly once asked: 'Why do mothers take their children to the supermarket to smack them?'

"Does he only chew when you're not paying attention to him?" I asked. "When you're watching television, for example."

"We have to keep our eye on him all the time," she replied. "But he's as good as gold in the house, he only chews when he's out."

It must be some sort of diet-related problem, I thought. Some dogs chew up sticks, or shred paper, probably in an attempt to increase their fibre intake. "Does he chew a lot of wood?" I asked.

"No," she said. "He likes playing with sticks, but I wouldn't say he chews them much."

"What about paper?" I asked. "Does he like shredding it or trying to shred other fibre-based material?"

"No," she replied. "Why do you ask that?"

"I'm trying to establish whether there's a diet link to his behaviour," I replied, but I was beginning to run out of ideas about why he was chewing. "What specifically is he chewing?" I asked.

"People."

"People? You mean mouthing their hands?"

"Well no, it's a bit more than that really."

"Is he hurting them?"

"Yes."

"You mean he's biting people?"

"Well yes, I suppose I do."

Incredible! A ten-minute conversation, during which time the word 'bite' never crossed her lips. This lady owned a dog with all the bite power of a hydraulic vice and which, apparently, was running around the local park like munch-man and she didn't want to admit it. Later that day, I was speaking to her vet on another matter and I relayed our conversation to him. He was totally surprised and had no idea the dog was aggressive to people, he too had only been told it was chewing.

Comment:

It's not surprising that people feel embarrassed when their dog develops a behaviour problem and, quite often, my clients live with a problem for a very long time. It's only when the problem starts to affect others that they have to face it and do something positive. By the time I actually saw this dog, he had bitten six people, the last of whom had reported the incident and the dog was then the subject of a court case. It was the police involvement that had prompted this owner to ask her vet for help, but even then, she would not admit what the real problem was.

WELL! HE DOESN'T BITE ME

Dateline: November 1993

My next remarkable clients were very typical of a lot I see from London. A well-dressed couple with a very expensive car; usually late arriving and with the lady holding a small obnoxious dog in her arms. On this occasion, it was a Dachshund and he had obviously read somewhere that the literal German translation was Badger Hound and viewed everyone he met as a badger. His name was Henry, but at first I thought that was the name of the lady's husband. As they followed me down to my office, I heard her say,
"Oh! Look Henry, they've got horses." Henry didn't reply.
"Look Henry, there's some more out there in the field."
This last remark made me turn round to see why Henry wasn't speaking and saw the lady holding the Dachshund high above her head so he could get a better view of the field. Her husband was following on behind with a resigned look on his face, looking for all the world like the modern hunter/gatherer male, pushing a trolley behind his wife in the supermarket.

When we got into the office, husband and wife sat on different sides of the room and the lack of eye contact, or any form of communication between them, was obvious. Henry was still being cradled in the woman's arms and, after I had supplied them each with a cup of coffee, during the course of which Henry gave me a very meaningful growl as I offered his mistress her cup, I suggested that she might like to put him on the floor so he could have a sniff around. Henry immediately ran over to where the man was sitting and stared at him in a very defiant manner. Having been ignored, he ran straight back to the woman and jumped on her lap, to which she responded by kissing the top of his head.
"So how can I help?" I asked.

"My husband is complaining that Henry keeps biting him," she said.

"It's not just me," he piped up. "It's anyone who gets near him."

"Oh, rubbish," she interrupted. "It's because people frighten him."

Henry certainly hadn't looked frightened when he had given her husband the challenging stare just a few moments previously.

"But darling," he complained. "Simone is living in fear of him."

"Well, I've told you before darling, if she acted more like a lady, instead of one of those horrid tomboy friends of hers, it wouldn't happen."

"She hasn't got any friends left now, thanks to your dog, or at least none that will come to the house," he said.

"Excuse me," I interjected, half to ask a question and half to remind them that I was still in the room. "Who's Simone?"

"Simone is our 11-year-old daughter," replied the lady.

"And Henry is biting her?" I asked. "Is he causing damage?"

"Yes he is!" replied the man. "She can't move without him attacking her."

"Oh, come off it darling," the woman interrupted again. "I think attacking her is a bit strong, they're only scratches."

"Well, she needed three stitches in the last scratch," he said in a rather sarcastic manner.

Things were starting to get a little heated and I was beginning to feel uncomfortable. Henry had obviously felt the tension, too, because he jumped off the woman's knee, gave the man another long defiant stare (to which the man looked away) and was now sniffing around my feet, adding further to my discomfort. He disappeared under my desk and I could hear him rooting through my waste-paper basket - I was not going to stop him.

"I can't see why everyone is making such a fuss," she said. "He's never bitten me and that's because I know how to treat him. If everyone else would just follow my example, they wouldn't have a problem."

Suddenly, Henry emerged from under my desk with a screwed-up letter in his mouth. He lay down facing me and started to shred it.

"If I tried to take that off him, what would he do?" I asked the lady.

"He'd bite you," she said with no hesitation.

"You don't see that as a problem?"

"No," she replied. "It's his bit of paper, he found it."

"But he found it in my basket, therefore it's my bit of paper and I might want it back," I said, beginning to feel stupid that I was arguing about a piece of paper.

"Well, you shouldn't have thrown it away," she said. "How is Henry supposed to know you wanted to keep it?"

I was rapidly beginning to understand her husband's resigned attitude and he was looking at me with a 'now you see what I have to live with' look on his face.

"If Henry was a Rottweiler, would you then see it as a problem?" I said in a triumphant manner - surely I'd got her now!

"No, I wouldn't," she replied. "The principle of finders-keepers still stands. But if Henry was a Rottweiler, I think it would be you that would see it as a problem," she added in the same triumphant way.

Comment:

These people did not require the services of a pet behaviour counsellor, a marriage guidance counsellor could have done them more good.

Clearly, Henry was being used as a catalyst for the problems they were having with their relationship and this is a situation which we see quite often. But what I found difficult to grasp, was that she was prepared to risk injury to her daughter in her efforts to keep this alliance with her dog against her husband.

No matter what advice I gave, this lady would have ignored it, and this is a potentially serious situation for people involved in the work that we do. If, following a visit to me, Henry had bitten Simone badly in the face, or anywhere else that could cause long term scarring, it could be claimed that it happened as a result of the advice I had given. It would be difficult to prove that the advice had been ignored, although I think I might have had some support from her husband. Nevertheless, it was a risk I was not prepared to take. Whenever children are at risk from dogs, I always err on the side of caution and my advice was for them to re-home Henry to a childless environment. I also recommended that his new owners should be made aware of the problem, so that they could take advice on how he should be treated from the outset. Basically, I believed that Henry was not really a bad dog, he was only reacting to his stressful environmental situation. As you can imagine, this advice went down like a lead balloon with the woman, but I definitely saw her husband perk up a notch.

In cases like this, I always ensure that my advice is well recorded. In this particular instance, I personally spoke to the referring vet, as well as sending him a detailed report. A copy of this report was also sent to the client, but I marked it clearly for the attention of the man. It hasn't happened yet, but I wonder if a pet dog's 'shrink' has ever been called as a witness in a divorce petition.

WOULDN'T YOU RUN AWAY?

Dateline: June 1988

It's not just ordinary pet folk who behave in such a manner that it makes you wish you were somewhere else; the nobility can do it just as well.

I was asked to visit an elderly Duchess, who was having problems with her Jack Russell. Sadly, the Duchess is no longer living, but I still feel that it would be a breach of client confidentiality to reveal her name. Her dog, however, was called Louis XIV, because it was the 14th Jack Russell she had owned. A brave lady; most people are cured of JR ownership after just one - I know, I've got one. The Duchess lived in a penthouse suite overlooking a large London park. It was a huge place, with a balcony that ran almost all the way round the top of the building. She lived in it with her little dog and a very elderly maid, who had been in her service since she was a little girl.

My first meeting with Louis took place in a hallway which was as long as a bowling alley. Along the length of both walls were placed high-backed, blue velvet-covered chairs, each with a royal coat of arms. Louis was using them to run up and down the hallway in a very excitable manner. Apparently, the chairs were from Westminster Abbey and were used at the coronation. I assume they were given to the Duchess - I mean I've heard of people taking towels from hotel rooms, but a lorry-load of royal chairs might have been noticed.

I was shown into the drawing room. The elderly maid followed us in and just stood there.

"Well," said the Duchess to the maid. "What do you want?"

"Would the gentleman like some coffee?" she replied.

"Would you like some coffee Mr. Fisher?" asked the Duchess.

"Thank you, Your Grace," I replied, and then turning my attention to the maid, I continued the sentence. "I would love a cup please."

"Yes, he'll take coffee," the Duchess said to the maid.

"Does he want normal or decaffeinated?" she asked the Duchess.

"Normal, or decaffeinated, Mr. Fisher?"

"Decaff please," I said, in the maid's direction.

"He'll have decaffeinated," said the Duchess to the maid.

I was beginning to understand the rules of this encounter by now; the maid does not talk to me and I should not to talk to her. It seemed to me to be quite a long-winded business, but it was obviously the correct protocol.

It was exactly at this point that I looked at Louis and I had to stifle my expression of amusement. He was laid with his paws crossed in a strategic position between the three of us and his head was swivelling towards whoever was talking at the time. He was obviously used to the whole scenario and was finding it as amusing as I was, but I bet he didn't feel as uncomfortable as I did.

"Would he like hot milk, or cold milk?" asked the maid.

"Hot or cold milk, Mr. Fisher?"

"Oh! Don't go to any bother, Your Grace. I'll have cold," I innocently replied.

"He'll have cold," the Duchess almost spat towards the maid. On that instant, I saw Louis's head grow 12 inches from his shoulders and swivel towards the maid. I remember thinking, he knows something I don't. I was right! The maid went ballistic.

"I've already heated the milk and now it will be wasted," she retorted in a very exasperated manner.

"Hot will be fine," I said, temporarily forgetting protocol by not waiting for my interpreter to speak first.

"No, it won't," said the obviously irate Duchess. "If he wants cold milk, he shall have cold milk. Go and get him coffee with cold milk."

"Well, I'm not drinking cold hot milk later," the maid spat back, as she stormed out of the room. I noticed that Louis followed her and I suspected that this milk saga had happened before and he was the one to benefit.

"She's quite mad, you know," said the Duchess. "I think she's going senile."

Not knowing what to reply, I decided not to and asked instead what the problem with Louis was.

"He won't come back to me," she replied.

No, I thought and I won't be in any rush, either. I asked whether he ran away, or whether he just wouldn't come close enough to be caught. She was very definite that he ran away. Just then, the maid returned, crashed the tray down on a table and walked out.

The Duchess had her coffee black and told me to help myself to milk. Just as well; the milk jug was warm and the milk inside it looked decidedly watery - like cold watery. Louis had returned with the maid, but had stayed where the milk jug was.

He looked really happy when I picked it up, and crestfallen when I poured some into my cup and put it down again. Isn't it funny, the little things behaviour counsellors pick up on?

Over coffee, we discussed Louis in some depth and I formed the opinion that we were really talking about a very bored dog. When given the chance to play with other dogs, he was going to seize that chance with all four paws. He was only 12 months old and, with all due respect to the Duchess, there was no way that she was nimble enough to cater for the activity levels of a dog at that age. She needed the constant support of a walking stick, which she probably didn't need when the other 13 Jack Russells were puppies. It was decided that we would take Louis to the park, so that I could witness his behaviour myself. I have to say that I steered the conversation in this direction, because I was worried that the maid might come back at any time to clear up and I wanted to be out of there before that happened.

Louis behaved like a perfect gentleman when his lead was being put on. He sat quietly on the lead, whilst the Duchess excused herself to go to the bathroom.

Whilst she was gone, the maid also broke protocol and said, "She's quite mad you know." I chose not to answer.

In the lift and across the lobby, Louis was extremely calm. Out in the road, he never attempted to pull, despite the fact that he obviously knew he was going to the park. The Duchess could only walk at a very slow pace for a few yards, before having to stop for a rest and Louis was fine about this. We passed about ten people, all of whom said, "Good morning, Your Grace. How's Louis today?"

That's fair enough, I thought, I don't expect people to wonder who the posh lady is walking with John Fisher, but I did wonder why Louis was so well known. I was to find out why, not much later.

As we arrived in the park, I saw Louis scan the horizon and as soon as the Duchess released him, he was off like a heat-seeking missile towards two dogs that were playing Frisbee with their owner 500 yards away.

"Louis darling," screamed the Duchess. "Come to mummy."

Do you think Louis took any notice of this? Not a chance! This was 'Louis

At Large' and he intended to remain at large until the park police picked him up in the lamp-post district. (The canine equivalent of the red light district!) As I set off to chase after him, the repeated call of, "Louis darling, come to mummy," echoed in my ears.

At one point, I almost got within ten yards of him, but he spotted another dog a quarter of a mile away and was gone. Eventually, I tricked him into coming close enough to be able to catch him, by making a fuss of another dog within his vision. This whole procedure took at least half an hour and throughout this time, I could hear the Duchess calling, "Louis darling, come to mummy."

Now I knew why Louis was so well known. Once back on the lead, Louis walked like a lamb to slaughter - totally resigned to the fact that he was being returned to a boring and unstimulating environment, where the highlight of the day would be whether some poor unsuspecting visitor asked for cold milk after the milk had already been boiled.

We arrived back at the penthouse and the Duchess rang the door bell. There was no reply, so she rang it again, this time for longer. Still no reply. I suggested that her maid might have gone out.

"She never goes out," the Duchess replied. "She's in there and she's refusing to answer the door."

Oh, no! Here we go again, I thought, as the Duchess pressed the bell and kept her finger on it.

"GO AWAY," shouted the maid from inside.

"I shan't go away! Open this door at once," the Duchess shouted back.

"I'm having my lunch."

"Open this door."

"I won't. You know what the doctor said. I'm not supposed to be running up and down - you always do this to me."

"Open the door, Mr Fisher wants a cup of coffee."

Oh no, he doesn't, thought Mr Fisher. He just wants to go home.

At this point, I noticed Louis was looking at me quite intently. If dogs could talk, he was clearly asking the question, 'Well, wouldn't you run away?'

Comment:

It is not unusual for elderly people who have owned a particular breed of dog for most of their lives to take on a new puppy too late in life and not be capable of satisfying their behavioural needs. Jack Russells are particularly active little dogs and if you don't give them things to do, they'll do things for themselves. This is exactly what was happening with Louis. Although I showed the Duchess some fun games that she could manage to play with him out on the huge balcony, which would add more stimulation to his life, it was impossible for her to organise physical activities for him in the park. Instead, with her grateful agreement, I arranged for a local dog walker to collect Louis every other day and take him for a good romp with three or four other friendly dogs.

DON'T ASK ME!

Dateline: August 1992

As a counsellor, public speaker and an author, it is not often I am lost for words, but sometimes people's attitudes to their pets leave me speechless. One such occasion happened at my London clinic, where all my appointments are made for me by the nurses and I have no idea until I get there just what problems I will be dealing with. I have to say that all the staff there are very helpful and generally screen all my clients for me, to make sure the problem is behavioural and not medical. (I have to say that, otherwise I'll be in trouble.) They explain the procedure for a behavioural consultation, length of time, costs and that it is a private, owner/counsellor/pet relationship. They also send out a pre-consultation questionnaire for the owner to complete at home and bring with them on the day. This gives me information about what the pet is doing, what it eats, where it sleeps etc. I prefer to have this information in front of me, rather than start off a consultation by asking a lot of questions. I consider formal note-taking on meeting someone for the first time as a bad counselling technique and I prefer a conversational start, with already prepared information to guide the discussion. As you can see, the whole process is very carefully thought-out to ensure that maximum information can be obtained, in the most relaxed manner. However, sometimes, the odd one slips through the safety net.

At the appointed time, I was standing in the waiting room when I saw a gleaming white Rolls Royce pull up outside. A very smartly dressed man got out, carrying a Shih Tzu - remember what I said about my London clients? He walked into the room and announced, to nobody in particular, that CoCo had an appointment with Mr Fisher. I introduced myself and invited him to follow me to my consulting room.

"Shall I wait here?" he asked.

"No, come through," I said, thinking he must have misunderstood what I had said the first time.

Once inside, he handed me the completed consultation form and asked if it was all right to put CoCo down on the floor.

"Sure," I said. "Let him have a sniff around, it will help to relax him. Dogs get very suspicious whenever they come to a veterinary surgery."

I had hurriedly checked the information sheet to establish whether CoCo was male or female - it's the only way to tell with a Shih Tzu, short of invading their privacy, when the name does not give you a clue,

"I see that CoCo doesn't like being left alone," I said, to start the conversation. "He destroys things like cushions and his own bedding, or any items of clothing he can get at?"

"He was very good in the car," the man replied.

I explained to him that this was usually the case. Many dogs who cannot be left alone at home, will quite happily sit in the car on their own, sometimes for long periods of time.

"Oh, no! He's not left in the car. Today was the first time he's been in it. That's why I say he was very good, it surprised me really," the man explained.

"I bet it worried you a bit as well," I replied, thinking about the Rolls outside. "I mean, if he's not been in it before, he might have done some damage, or been sick on the seats."

"Oh, it doesn't matter about that," he replied.

Rich B.....d! I thought.

"Is he a very attached dog?" I asked, hurriedly putting my envious thoughts to one side. "Does he follow you around a lot?"

"Well, not me, he doesn't, but he quite likes the wife. She has more to do with him than me."

"I see he's exercised twice a day. Do you ever take him out?"

"No, this is the first time he's been with me," he replied.

What a funny relationship, I thought. Perhaps having a Shih Tzu is just another status symbol - like the car - and he thinks as little of it as the vehicle. "Couldn't your wife come today?" I asked, beginning to wonder why her husband had come.

"No, she's working," he said. "Anyway, she wouldn't have wanted to."

This consultation was getting stranger by the minute. Dogs that destroy things when they're left alone, especially items of clothing, are usually suffering from a separation anxiety caused by an over attachment to their owners. I was starting to doubt that this was the case because clearly this man and his wife had no real bond with CoCo. I was also rapidly going off this man, not only because of his attitude to the dog, but because I had a mental image of his wife doing other people's washing, so that he could drive around in a Rolls Royce all day.

"I see he's fed twice a day," I read from the form. "What is he fed on?"

"I don't know," he replied.

"Do you know if he eats well?" I asked, trying not to let sarcasm burst through.

"I don't know," he said. "I'm never there."

"Where does he sleep?" I asked.

"I don't know," said the man.

"You don't know where he sleeps?" I asked incredulously.

"Well, why should I?" he asked. "I'm only the chauffeur!"

Comment:

Fancy sending your dog off with the chauffeur to see a shrink. What did they expect me to do? Perhaps they thought I would lie CoCo down on a couch and ask him if his mother was cruel to him, or whether he had been abused as a puppy. Of course, we don't do that. Anyway, dogs are not allowed on the couch. This man's whole attitude, starting with his question about staying in the waiting room, fell into place as soon as he made that statement and I felt slightly guilty about my feelings towards him. His wife was the house keeper and both of them had thought that I would need to see the owners, and found it strange when he was asked to bring the dog himself. He promised to report back to his employers and get them to make another appointment when they could bring CoCo. To this day, I have never heard a word from them, but at least the chauffeur paid for the appointment.

TWO MOMENTS OF PANIC.

Dateline: May 1994

This next incident happened at one of my other veterinary clinics. Seeing cases within a veterinary establishment is slightly different to seeing them at my practice headquarters in Surrey. In a veterinary surgery, a lot of the dogs are stressed and frightened, simply because they are 'at the vets'. Once they realise that this is not a normal consultation and people are not advancing upon them brandishing hypodermic needles, they relax a bit. My Surrey practice is quite different - there are not the smells, or the familiar medicine cabinets consistent with a veterinary practice and so the dog is usually more relaxed from the outset. When a dog, or any other mammal for that matter (including the human mammal) is frightened, there are four strategies we can adopt. We can FIGHT - become aggressive, we can take FLIGHT - run away, we can FIDDLE ABOUT - appease and try to deflect the potential threat, or we can FREEZE - stay perfectly still and hope that the threat will go away. If you are walking through a totally dark room and you suddenly hear a strange sound, it is the latter survival mode that you are likely to adopt, until your brain has collected more information about what to do next. Depending upon the type of dog I am seeing and its early experiences with fearful situations, it is not unusual for me to see one of these strategies for survival at the start of a consultation. Because of the in-depth nature of such a consultation, it is impossible to do one properly in less than one-and-a-half, to two hours. That is unless you find out fairly early on that it's the chauffeur who's brought the dog.

On this particular day, my first consultation had been concluded very quickly and I was in the rest room having a cup of coffee. One of the nurses came in to tell me that my next client had arrived early and asked me whether

I was prepared to see her straight away. I told her that I would and followed her out in the direction of my consulting room. As we walked there, she said, "The lady has gone to the toilet, but the dog's in there tied to the radiator. I've given it some biscuits, but it's not eaten them. I think it's a bit frightened."

I entered the room and saw an elderly Pekingese lying down, with three bone-shaped biscuits right in front of its nose. It was not moving a muscle. That's a very frightened dog, I thought, and my interest in behaviour instantly diagnosed a FREEZE mode strategy. I decided to ignore the dog, because approaching a frightened animal is only going to increase the level of fear. I sat down and started to conclude my notes from the last consultation.

After about five minutes, the owner had not returned from the toilet and the dog had still not moved. This was unusual - not the amount of time ladies spend in the bathroom - but the amount of time an animal will stay in freeze after their brain has registered that there is no immediate threat. I decided to try and make contact with the dog.

"It's OK puppy," I said. I call all dogs 'puppy'; it means I don't have to remember their names.

"No needles today."

There was absolutely no response from the dog.

"Don't you like boring old dog biscuits," I said, in a coochy-coo type of voice. "How about some choc drops?" I reached for my supply. Still no response.

I approached the dog carefully to offer the more rewarding tit-bit and noticed that its eyes were totally glazed over. I became a bit concerned and looked at it in more detail - it wasn't breathing!

CHRIST! I thought. IT'S DEAD! What am I going to tell the owner? I know, I'll say that when I entered the room the dog lunged at me and being tied to the radiator, the collar must have broken its neck. No, that won't work, it's not big enough to do that. I know, I'll say it came at me with a knife and I had to defend myself. Don't be stupid, Fisher, get a grip on yourself. I know! I'll hide one of the biscuits and say it must have choked itself.

Just then, I heard giggling coming from the waiting room.

In an instant, the whole scenario came to me. I had been 'set up' by the nurses. The dog was dead on arrival and had been put into my empty consulting room prior to disposal.

I rushed out of the room, trying to put my best panic face on and shouted, "Quick! Somebody help! The dog is staggering about and making choking noises."

"Oh, s**t!" said one of the nurses. "It wasn't dead."

Three of them rushed into my room, with a total look of panic on their faces. Of course, the dog was where they had left it, but I had the satisfaction of turning the panic tables.

Comment:

Working as I do in a predominantly veterinary environment, I have developed an enormous amount of respect for the profession. On a daily basis, they are faced with having to put much-loved animals to sleep, which to an animal lover is not easy - and it is their love for animals which makes them want to enter the profession in the first place. Not only that, they also have to cope with the grieving clients and, in this respect, they have all developed counselling skills in their own right.

Very few people who are locked into their own grief at the time consider how upsetting it is for the veterinary staff as well, but they are the ones who have to put a brave face on it and comfort the client. With this amount of daily pressure, it's no wonder that the veterinary profession has a high incidence of suicide. Light relief is an essential coping strategy. I say this to reassure readers that death is not taken lightly, but sometimes you have to be able to laugh to enable yourself to cope with it.

FORMING A BOND

Dateline: January 1988

The following case is one I have reported before in one of my other books, but it was so bizarre, it warrants inclusion in 'Dotty Dogs'. It involves a young couple with a small baby and a two-year-old Boxer dog called Sam.

On the first occasion when I saw Sam, the woman brought him on her own. Her husband was away at sea, but while he had been home for Christmas there had been three or four incidents where Sam had growled at him quite meaningfully. Basically, the man was frightened of dogs. The couple had bought Sam as a puppy to try and help him overcome this fear and he and the dog had developed quite a good relationship. Just before Christmas, the baby was born and it was after this that the problem started. Because of his fear of dogs, whenever Sam growled at him, it was his wife that punished him by biting his ear - a brave and slightly stupid lady, who obviously believed the old wives' tale that this is the best way to punish a dog. When a dog with the jaw power of a Boxer threatens to bite, the last thing you want to do is to put your face close to his and bite his ear. It was a tribute to Sam's temperament that she got away with it.

However, her husband's parting words as he left to rejoin his ship were; "Get the dog cured, or get rid of it." She was left in no doubt that if Sam continued to be aggressive, either he would have to go, or her husband would leave her. This is an ultimatum that I hear reported many times and it is a dangerous one to issue. Some people work on the principle that you can always get another partner, but a good dog is hard to find.

It is interesting for me to report this case again eight years later, because although the advice I gave then would not have altered much, the reasons behind the advice would have done. In those days, it was vogue in behaviour therapy to look at things in terms of rank and I diagnosed the problem as one of dominance aggression. In his master's absence, the dog had become the high-ranking male in the home and was objecting to the return of a rival male. The advice I gave was to reduce his rank below everyone else in the house by restricting his privileges. This meant not allowing him in certain rooms, especially the master bedroom, not allowing him to push through doorways, not allowing him on the furniture, etc. Nowadays, we tend to look at things more in terms of control of resources and are more specific about the things that dogs should and should not be allowed to take for granted.

Instead of viewing our relationship with our dogs as a rank struggle, we now see that we are one of the resources to be competed for, rather than something to compete against. If I saw this case again today, I would be far more investigative about the circumstances of the aggressive encounters and instead of advising a blanket restriction on Sam's daily activities, I would give more specific advice around the areas that aggression was likely to occur. Had I done that then, I would have correctly diagnosed the problem on the first visit, rather than on the second visit, where the case went in a whole new, and very strange, direction.

I received a phone call some weeks later to say that this lady's husband was home and that Sam was terrifying him, to the point where he had shut himself in the kitchen when she went shopping one day. He was demanding that Sam had to be put down, but at the end of the call, they both agreed to come and see me, to give Sam one last chance.

When they arrived, they had the baby with them and we were only a little way into the consultation when the baby started to cry. Sam immediately became very agitated and started to jump up on the woman, as if trying to get on her lap. Her husband stood up, presumably to call Sam off her, but Sam made it absolutely clear that he should sit down again, which he did, very quickly. I must admit, so would I - Sam left no one in any doubt that he meant SIT!

The woman managed to control Sam, but he remained very agitated over the baby crying. Eventually, she had to put him back in the car, because it was becoming impossible for us to carry on a conversation and her husband was becoming increasingly frightened. When she returned, she explained that the reason why he suddenly started to behave like that was because the baby was hungry and Sam usually got shut away, because the baby was breast fed.

"What difference does that make," I innocently asked.
"Because he tries to push the baby out of the way," she replied.
"Why should he do that?" I asked. "He doesn't cause a problem with the baby at other times, does he?"
"Oh, no! He's really good with her, it's just that I have an excess of milk and the midwife said that if I give it to the dog, it will help to form a bond between him and the baby."

Before any new mothers rush off to feed the dog, let me assure you, this is just not true. I suppose you could call it 'an old midwives' tale', but this is probably unfair. I have no doubt that if this comment was made, it was made as a joke. If it was a serious comment, then no doubt the midwife meant that she should express the milk, before giving it to the dog. Clearly, Sam's owner had not understood it this way.

Comment:
I have no comment. I'm still in shock eight years later.

FORMING AN EVEN CLOSER BOND

If you've recovered from the shuddering thought of someone breast feeding an adult male Boxer, read on - but I warn you, there's more to come.

Dateline: July 1994

Bert was a four-year-old male Dobermann, who was presented by a married couple. The man looked decidedly uncomfortable about having to come. Wherever possible, I try to persuade the whole family to attend, but it still tends to be predominantly women who present their pets for treatment. The problem they had stated on their form was that Bert was 'chasing dragonflies'. A short seasonal problem, I thought, considering our English summers. If I can keep them talking long enough, the problem should cure itself. But there was more to it than that.

The woman stated that Bert was a wonderful companion, with no aggressive streaks at all, but when he met other four-legged creatures (I presumed she meant dogs), he became so excited that he was a nuisance to other owners. Because of this, they could not let him off the lead, but he had the run of their very large garden, in which there were two huge ponds. By chasing dragonflies, he had ripped the lining of one of these ponds and was in danger of doing the same to the other. After these chases, he became extremely hyper and uncontrollable. He also suffered from eczema, which was made worse by constantly being damp. Well, I thought, that was nicely abbreviated into 'chasing dragonflies'.

"He licks himself a lot," she added to her long list of problems. "You know, down there," and nodded her head towards the floor.
The man stirred uncomfortably in his chair.

"Are you sure he's not flank sucking?" I asked. "Dobermanns are renowned for that particular behaviour trait."

"Oh, it's not his leg. It's his penis that he's licking," she replied.

The man was obviously beside himself with embarrassment and when people feel embarrassed, they often make witty comments in an effort to hide their feelings.

"Wish I could do it," he muttered.

I resisted the urge to tell him that if he offered the dog a biscuit, he might let him, and continued talking to the woman.

"I wouldn't worry too much about that," I said. "Lots of dogs do it. If you were to ask me why, I would have to say it's because they can - it's normal behaviour."

"I wouldn't say it was normal, the amount of time he spends doing it," she stated.

"Well perhaps, considering his medical history of eczema, he might have an infection or an irritation. I should get your vet to check it out," I suggested. I wanted to get her off the subject of penis licking and had just nicely bounced the ball back into the vet's side of the court.

In my opinion, the real problem was Bert's total lack of control and I wanted to steer the conversation back in that direction.

"What sort of formal training has Bert had?" I asked. "Have you ever attended any training classes with him?"

Her husband looked very relieved that the subject had been changed, but his relief was to be short-lived.

"Yes, we went to dog training, but they asked us to stop going because Bert was too disruptive in the class. But getting back to his licking, he does it sometimes until he reaches climax. I think he's frustrated. Is that possible?"

The man had his head in his hands by this time and I could tell he just wanted the earth to swallow him up.

"Well, perhaps you can talk to your vet about that as well," I suggested. "Maybe he will suggest having Bert neutered, which will probably be for the best if its causing problems," I replied. Secretly, I was thinking - Jeez! This woman's got a fetish.

"But is it possible that he's frustrated?" she continued.

"Well, I wouldn't have thought so, but if he is, organising some things for him to do might help - you know, like mentally stimulating games to play."

"Oh! I do stimulate him," she replied.

"How do you do that?" I asked. Her husband groaned and I got the feeling that I shouldn't have asked that question.

"I give him hand relief," she said. "Is that wrong?"

It's not part of my job description to moralise about how people live with their animals, and by now, I was feeling as uncomfortable as her husband.

"I don't suppose it's doing him any good," I feebly replied.

"But is it harming him?" she asked.

"Well, I don't suppose it's doing him any harm either," I replied.

"See, George," she said to her husband. "I told you if I asked him, he'd say it wasn't doing any harm."

Now I know why her husband had looked so uncomfortable from the start, he knew what was coming - or is that the wrong phrase to use?

Comment:

Incredible as it might seem, this case and the one before it, prove that occasionally people's relationship with their pets goes beyond the bounds of normal behaviour. I really didn't know what to say to this woman, so I chose the easy option and changed the subject. Besides, who was I to spoil her Saturday night's entertainment? I did think later, when I was relaying the story to my disbelieving wife - it gives a whole new meaning to the traditional dog training command for a recall.

WHERE THERE'S A WILL, THERE'S A WORRY

Dateline: February 1987

Miss Gort was a very frail lady in her late sixties or early seventies. She had made the appointment to come and see me in Surrey, because her dog was aggressive to people it didn't know. Not an unusual case, except Rudi, as her dog was called, was a massive male Rottweiler and on top of that, he didn't know me.

I heard her car pull up on our shingle car park and gave her a few minutes, before going out to meet her. As I arrived in the car park, I was met by the sight of a spitting, frothing, snarling beast of a dog, who, although we hadn't met before, had obviously heard of me and had the full intention of showing me that I had met my match at last. The only thing stopping me from experiencing Rudi's Rottie wrath was a lead, wrapped around an elderly lady's wrist, who in turn was desperately trying to hang on to the tail-gate of her car. As we were on icy shingle, she was having a job to keep on her feet and there was absolutely no way she could let go of the car with me stood there - Rudi was not bluffing. Drawing on all my years of experience, I very quickly diagnosed that this was not a good scene and decided to go to the office and let her follow me later. Over the noise that Rudi was making, I told her to follow the fence down the drive, and that my office was the converted end stable. I resisted the urge to make my usual comment - that there are two stables in the world where miracles happen and the other was in Jerusalem - even though I thought it would be a miracle if I didn't get bitten that day.

By making sure that I was in the office first, Rudi would be coming on to my territory, instead of me invading his. This had obviously added to his anger, because I had approached his car. I was hoping, no, I was praying, that this might take some of the sting out of the temper tantrum I had just witnessed. My wife told me later that she had feared for my safety when she watched Miss Gort slowly make her way to my office. She grabbed a fence post and regained her balance, before making a lunge for the next post. This procedure got her down the drive. To get past the stables, she grabbed the door frame of each open-top door. Rudi weighed in at around 120 pounds and she weighed around 90.

The pair eventually burst through my doorway and Rudi looked at me as if to say; 'Oh, it's you again is it? I thought you had run away once.'
My ploy had worked though; he was marginally calmer.
Since seeing Rudi all those years ago, my office has been extended to twice the size and I now have very firmly secured hooks in the walls. On this day, I was in a room 12 foot by 12 foot, with 120 pounds of angry Rottweiler and only a frail old lady as an anchor point. I remember thinking; remind me again John, why do I do this for a living?

Having got seated, Rudi calmed down a bit, but he never once took his eyes off me. I actually like Rottweilers and don't believe they deserve the reputation that often goes before them, but they do have an unnerving ability to fix you with an expressionless stare. I avoided eye contact with him and proceeded to subtly try and establish why such an elderly lady would want to own a dog of this size and sheer power. To cut a long and very frightening consultation short, Miss Gort had been the house keeper for a retired army officer. He had recently died and, in his will, he had left Rudi to her care, with a large amount of money to ensure that he got the best of everything. She was obeying his instructions and feeding Rudi on the best cuts of raw meat that money could buy. Among a variety of other problems that we needed to deal with, this dog was out of his head on raw meat protein and a totally unbalanced diet.

At one point, Miss Gort was sat on the edge of a leather-covered settee, holding on to Rudi's lead with both hands. I stood up to make us both a cup of coffee and Rudi lunged at me, dumping Miss Gort unceremoniously face down on her knees and elbows - but she managed to hang on to the lead. We were in a stalemate situation. I was trapped in a corner with Rudi's hot breath almost in my face and with Miss Gort hanging on for grim death but unable to get up. I started praying for the second time that day, because I was absolutely certain that Rudi had not rushed over to help with the coffee cups. After what seemed like an eternity, my wife walked past the open-top door, which distracted Rudi sufficiently for me to escape. The slippy leather settee has since been changed.

I've seen a lot of angry dogs since that day and had a lot of hairy moments, but none have compared to my meeting with Rudi. Without doubt, it was the most frightening consultation I have ever conducted.

Comment:

Rudi responded very well and very quickly to a variety of procedures which we put into place. A head collar for greater control and to save Miss Gort's arms from being ripped off her body. Some of the money was used to employ an experienced dog walker and trainer to give Rudi more off-territory exercise and greater mental stimulation. More importantly, he was put on a well-balanced diet and this produced almost immediate improvement. Without doubt, diet is a major player where aggressive behaviour is concerned, although, at the time of writing, there is no scientific evidence to back up this statement. Horse people have known about the diet-behaviour link for years and, for that matter, so have boxers. When boxers prepare for title fights, they eat a predominantly meat diet - it gives them the fizz needed to keep the aggression going. Perhaps Frank Bruno should have eaten American beef before his Tyson fight - not British.

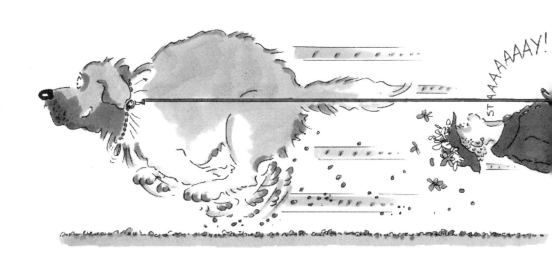

A SEVERE DOSE OF GRAVEL RASH

Dateline: September 1987

It never ceases to amaze me just how mismatched some people and their dogs are. OK, the Duchess could physically restrain her dog and Miss Gort's dog was bequeathed to her, rather than her choosing to own it, but the lady in this case purposely selected the breed she was having a problem with.

I received a phone call from a lady who had been a life-long friend of the late, famous TV dog trainer, Barbara Woodhouse. Throughout their friendship, she had been involved in helping Barbara to train dogs and other animals for TV and films, but she desperately needed help with her three-year-old male St Bernard, who was showing aggression to some people and attacked all dogs on sight. I mention the friendship with Barbara, merely to point out that this lady was no slouch when it came to making sure that dogs knew their place and when I met her, she was definitely a chip off the old block.

I was with another client when she arrived and my wife suggested that she exercise her dog in the paddock. When she came to tell me that she had arrived, she added, "You're not going to believe what you see." She was right. When I went out to introduce myself, I was faced with the sight of an 11-stone St Bernard, wearing a Barbara Woodhouse choke chain. Attached to this was a 25-foot-long horse's lunge rein, partially gathered up in the hands of a nine-stone elderly lady, with the other end tied around her waist. They were on the other side of the paddock when I arrived and the dog spotted me before the owner and charged towards me barking furiously. Taken completely by surprise, the line was yanked out of her hands and her waist was exposed to the full force of an 11-stone dog travelling at speed.
Now, you don't need a degree in engineering to work out what happened

next. You're right! She was yanked off the ground, like a cork popping out of a bottle of bubbly and dragged across the paddock like a water skier without skis. Slightly less audible than the dog, was the owner's frantic shout of "STAAAAY." Once again, my years of experience with aggressive dogs saved me from being bitten or flattened - I ran like hell and managed to slam the paddock gate shut on him, with me on the safe side.

So started another one of those strange consultations, which, you are probably beginning to realise, I get from time to time.

The lady obviously had a pre-conceived idea that I was going to TRAIN her dog to behave properly. It doesn't happen so much now, but a few years ago, many of my clients turned up in their 'dog training' gear, not having the slightest notion of what a behaviour consultation was all about. It was evident that she couldn't understand why I was sitting down making notes, instead of plodding up and down the paddock shouting, "HEEL, DOWN, STAY." Training this dog in its current frame of mind was doomed to failure and deep down in her mind, I think she knew it. She had tried and failed. So had a top visiting American trainer who had been taught personally by Barbara Woodhouse. However, I suspect she couldn't see what we were doing was going to get us anywhere either.

Suddenly, she jumped up from her seat and announced, "WATCH THIS!" She rushed out of the room, clutching her lunge line and headed towards the paddock. I followed her, rapidly forming the opinion that I was losing control of the meeting. Once in the paddock, she took hold of the lunge line at about the length of a normal lead, leaving the rest draped behind her, but still tied to her waist.

"WALKIES!" she shouted at the top of her voice, which I noticed made my neighbour look up from his vegetable plot. Oh God, I thought, he'll think I told her to shout that.

YANK went the lead, but the dog never moved an inch. Suddenly, it shot off at right angles to her, pulling the lead out of her hands again, and cocked his leg against the nearby fence.

It's just as well the fence is closer than the total length of that line, I thought, Otherwise she would have been paddock skiing again. I thought too soon. He suddenly made a run for the gate, but the route he took was behind where she was standing.

"STAAAAAY!" she shouted again.

Too late! She did the most spectacular pirouette, before hitting the deck again - the dog just ran as if she wasn't there. This time, I opened the gate to protect her. Unless she followed directly in his wake through the gate, she was going to go through the wire I had dog-proofed my paddock rails with, like cheese through a grater. Not to be deterred, she picked herself up, dusted her clothes, gathered up the line, told the dog he was in serious trouble, gave his neck another enormous yank, demanded him to, "WALKIES!" and set off down the fence line.

This time, the dog went with her - for about ten feet. Then he stopped and cocked his leg again. I noticed my neighbour had stopped gardening altogether and was watching all of this in obvious amusement.

Yank went the chain on his neck and cock went his leg.

"Stop doing that!" she shouted.

"WALKIES!" YANK. She was determined that she was going to show me and him who was the boss, but both me and him knew she was going to fail. All of this commotion brought my neighbour's little Border-cross-Jack

Russell Terrier out to see what was going on and the St Bernard spotted it through the fence at the same time as the woman did.

"NOOOO!" she shouted, before going on one of her little trips again. I thought it was a good time to suggest coffee.

The amount of times he had cocked his leg prompted me to suggest that she have him neutered, but she told me that it had been done 18 months ago and it had made no difference. I was beginning to despair for a solution. From the little bit of information that I had managed to glean from her, I knew that, providing I could overcome her years of indoctrination into how dogs should be fed, exercised, lived with etc, we would make progress on the level of aggression, but how to give her physical control, in order to stop the regular exposure to severe bouts of gravel rash, was another problem. She was quite adamant that she had to keep him tied to her waist, even if it was only effective in slowing him down a bit to give the other dog a chance to get away. I decided to take the bull by the horns and suggest that a Barbara Woodhouse disciple should consider trying to walk him on a head collar. To my complete surprise, she agreed.

Luckily, I had one big enough to fit the dog's huge head and he accepted it as if he had worn one all his life. After only two attempts at trying to dictate the direction in which they were walking, he walked alongside her like a lamb. We exposed him, at a safe distance, to other people and dogs and he made no attempt to go for them. What was remarkable about his almost immediate transformation, was that he made no attempt to cock his leg. With the fun over, my neighbour went back to his garden.

Comment:
The old style of yank and stomp training is rapidly being rejected in favour

of more inducive, reward-based methods. Certainly, in behaviour therapy, force is not a technique which is ever considered, usually because it has already been tried before the client is referred. This case really highlighted the futility of trying to force an animal that is stronger than us. Every attempt by his owner to physically control him had proved ineffective and each time she tried, it just proved to him that he was superior to her. Perhaps the resulting quick squirt of urine was the canine equivalent of 'UP YOURS'!

ARE THERE ANY PROBLEMS IN THE BEDROOM?

Dateline: September 1995

Following are two cases and what makes them unusual, is that I saw them one after the other on the same day. Both sets of owners made the same comments about how good their dogs were usually and, except for the problem that they were reporting, they both described their dogs as perfect pets. If these are perfect pets, then as a colleague of mine would say - my bum's a biscuit!

CASE ONE.

This concerned an elderly London couple, who owned a seven-year-old Border Terrier called Deefor. Get it? D for Dog. Deefor had been referred because, in one evening, while his owners were at a restaurant, Deefor had caused £8000 worth of damage to furniture, carpets, curtains and clothes in their home. The actual type of damage was not inconsistent with a dog in a state of panic because it had been left 'home alone', it's just that everything in their London home was very expensive. The couple were deeply shocked when they returned on this particular evening because, as they stated, Deefor had never done anything like this before.

There was, in fact, a very good reason why he had never done this before - he had never been left alone before - not at any time. Deefor went on holiday with them. If they visited friends he went with them. If they went shopping, to the theatre, or to a restaurant, he stayed in the car. On the evening in question, they were being chauffeur driven and they never gave a second thought about leaving Deefor at home. I suppose, because he had never caused a problem when they left him in the car, they had no reason to suspect there would be one at home.

As is usual in these cases, the cure is to gradually condition the dog towards a relationship which is less attached, or less dependent, upon the owners. These dogs generally follow their owners around the house and have virtually 24-hour contact with them. Deefor was no exception and, not only did he sleep in their bedroom, he shared their bed with them. Not on it - in it! When I told them that the long-term aim was to get Deefor to accept sleeping in his own bed in another room, I was told that this would not be possible. The owners had tried this before for other reasons and he just screamed the place down, which was unfair on the neighbours. It was at this stage they described more fully what they had previously called their perfect pet.

Apparently, for the last three years, the man had been having trouble with a weak bladder and could not go through the night without visiting the bathroom. His wife had a problem sleeping and needed to take pills every night, which meant she could not be woken up. When the man came back from the bathroom, Deefor would not let him get back into bed and had bitten him on more than a few occasions. The problem had got so bad, that he no longer even attempted to return to his own bed, but slept in the spare room. Because of his perfect pet, this man spent the first part of the night with his wife and his dog and the second part on his own in another room.

CASE TWO.

Half an hour later, I was talking to a young couple with a ten-month-old male German Shepherd Dog. The man was a big strapping rugby player, and his wife ran a business from home. They were complaining about their dog barking at the front gate when they let it have the run of the garden. Even though they gave the dog three good walks a day, they felt it was a shame not to let him take advantage of such a big garden when the weather was fine. In every other respect - you've guessed it - he was the perfect pet.

I had noticed when they arrived, that the dog was a bit on the thin side. His coat was also a bit dull and my other enquiries led me to the conclusion that a change of diet would benefit this dog, not necessarily for the sake of his behaviour, but more especially for his long-term good health. I was making a list of his daily nutritional intake, including snacks and tit-bits, when the man suddenly remembered something.

"Oh yes, and just before we go to bed, he gets three bone-shaped biscuits which we hide for him in the kitchen."
"That's wonderful," I said. "I wish more people would do things like that. Instead of just giving the dog something for nothing, getting them to earn rewards is a great way of improving your relationship. It's especially good that you make him earn it in such a stimulating way. By hiding the food, you are exercising his foraging and hunting instincts and with the tremendous ability that dogs have to detect scent, there can't be a better way to earn a reward. Well done! You both get extra brownie points in my book."
It was quite a speech.

The man was looking at me as if I was quite mad.
"Is there anything wrong?" I asked.
"Well, no. Not really," he replied. "Except we don't do it for that reason."
"Why do you do it then?" I enquired.
"If he gets into the bedroom before I do, he won't let me in."

Comment:
It's amazing how people organise their lives around a problem, especially in

the latter case. Here we had a young, very powerful animal that was challenging his owner for bedroom rights, yet they complained that he barked at the front gate. It is not unusual for my clients to tell me something that their dog does, but which they totally accept. Quite often, what they accept as normal behaviour is far more serious than the problem they are reporting. I suppose what is a problem to one person, is not necessarily a problem to another. I know this to be true because people often ring me up to say that their dog is doing so and so, and I think to myself, so what, so does mine.

THE DANGEROUS DOGS ACT - A SERIOUS NOTE

It is a sad fact that since the introduction of the Dangerous Dogs Act in 1991, the biggest file in my office is for court cases. I am frequently asked to assess the behaviour and temperament of a dog which has fallen foul of Section Three of this ill-thought out Act and usually to appear in court as an expert witness. In fact, I am sitting in a solicitor's room at a Magistrates court at this very moment, writing this on my lap top, whilst waiting to give evidence. The majority of people think that the DDA is about Pit Bull Terriers and other alleged fighting breeds and that it doesn't apply to ordinary pet dog owners. Wrong! Section Three of the Act reads as follows:

Sub-section (1) Creates an offence applying to any dog which is dangerously out of control in a public place. The offence applies to both the owner and, if different, the person who was in charge of the dog at the time. If, as a consequence of the dog being out of control, it injures any person, an aggravated offence is committed.

It goes on to say.

By reference to case law, the term 'injury' does not necessarily require physical contact, and can include shock.

Think about that for a moment. Any ordinary pet dog can rush up to someone barking and if that person claims to have been frightened, or shocked by the incident, they can choose to report it to the police. If they do, the owner runs the risk of being prosecuted and, if they can't prove their innocence, they are guilty of a criminal offence. A far fetched example? Not so; the case I am waiting to appear in concerns a dog which was on the lead when it bit another dog that ran underneath its legs. It also frightened the person who was in charge of the dog that was bitten.

A criminal offence?! My Jack Ratweiler, Chip, (a 14-year-old, totally deaf Jack Russell, who's only as big as a rat, but thinks she's a Rottweiler), owns the lane outside our house - well, she thinks she does. Nobody is allowed to use the lane without her express permission and she lies in wait behind a hedge in our car park for trespassers. She waits until they have gone past and then rushes up behind them shouting, 'GO AWAY, GO AWAY, GO AWAY'! She's done it for 12 years and people just say, "Good morning Chip," but strictly speaking, I run the risk of being reported. I've reported her myself three times, but they won't lock her up.

Readers might be shocked to hear that someone like me should have a dog who behaves like that, but my excuse is that I have trained my dogs to be problem dogs so that I can better understand other people's problems - and I'm sticking to that excuse.

Under this piece of legislation, not only does it mean that if a dog behaves like a dog the owner can be prosecuted, but there are two worrying aspects to the way the Act has been worded.
1. Unlike the great tradition that you are innocent until proven guilty, guilt is assumed in the DDA and you have to prove otherwise.
2. If an aggravated injury is caused, the magistrates have no options open to them other than to order that the dog be destroyed. They cannot apply common sense, they cannot order that the dog be kept on a lead or muzzled in a public place, they can only order death.

I am not saying that all dogs should be saved. If a dog is dangerous and out of control then it should be euthanased, but the 1871 Control of Dogs Act is still on the statute book and is perfectly adequate for dealing with this problem. What this Act does however, is allow the magistrates to consider the grey areas and hand down sensible judgements. At the time of writing, there is a great deal of pressure being put on the government to amend the DDA, but this pressure has been applied for some years now and they still won't yield. I hope by the time this book is being read, things will be different.

P.S. As a matter of interest, the owner of the dog in the case I have just been involved with has been found not guilty of the offence. Nevertheless, it must be quite a shock for a usually law-abiding citizen to find themselves in the dock for a day and have to be granted bail, so that they can go out for something to eat at lunch time.

That's it! Off my soap box. I mention all of this as a forerunner to the next diary entry, which goes to show that it is not all gloom and doom.

LET'S PLAY

Dateline: July 1993

Lucy was the sweetest, people loving, six-year-old Staffordshire Bull Terrier bitch that you could ever meet. She lived with her owner, Kate and her 12-year-old daughter Anne and they had obtained Lucy from a friend when she was just an eight-week-old puppy. She was a very much loved family pet. When she entered my office, she gave me an, 'OOH! Goody, a new person' look, and came straight towards me with her bum nearly wagging her back legs off the floor. The reason she had been brought to me was because she was accused of being a dangerous dog.

There is one sure-fire thing about the behaviour of Staffies, and that is, they all have a stick fetish. For some reason, they love to have a stick in their mouth and usually, the bigger the better. If they are dangerous at all, it is that they are likely to break your leg as they go running past you with half a tree in their mouth. If you visit the local park and look across the playing fields, you will see dogs of all different breeds, but you won't see a Staffie. Look up in the trees however, and there they are, hundreds of them, all hanging on to the branches. Lucy was no exception and outside Kate's house was a great pile of sticks, because Lucy brought one back from every walk. Because she liked sticks, this had been encouraged as a game, which both Kate and Anne played with her at every opportunity and had done so ever since she was a puppy. So had every visitor who came to the house, or every friend that they met on a walk. Lucy was put on this earth just to carry sticks.

In July 1992, Kate had taken Lucy to the shops and had tied her up outside a newsagent's. Somehow, the lead had come undone and just then, an old man walked by, leaning heavily on a walking stick. Yes, you're ahead of me again. Lucy grabbed the stick and the man started to play with her - well, that must be what Lucy thought, because he started pulling on the stick. During this tug of war, the man fell over and unfortunately, broke his hip. According to witnesses, at this point Lucy let go and when Kate came out of the shop, she was just sitting looking puzzled, while three or four people were tending to the man. The police swooped and unloaded the full power of the Dangerous Dogs Act.

Of course, Lucy passed her assessment with flying colours, during which I entered my office with a walking stick. Lucy grabbed it without hesitation and she was not going to let go easily, but she was certainly only playing. I conditioned her to a sound avoidance procedure, using a product known as 'Dog Training Discs' and very soon, Lucy wouldn't even look at a walking stick, let alone try to grab one. I needed to do this so that I could reassure the court that the chance of a repeat incident was highly unlikely. I was also able to explain that, had there been any aggressive or predatory intent on Lucy's behalf, when the man fell over, she would have attacked him. Instead, she sat down and was highly confused by the whole affair.

The court case was eventually listed for September 1993, almost 15 months after the incident. During this time, the worry that they would have to put Lucy to sleep, made Kate ill and affected Anne's school work. The day before I was due in court, the solicitor rang to say that the prosecution had read the case notes, in particular my report, and were not offering any evidence.

Lucy lived and Kate and Anne were highly emotional with relief and very grateful to me. Their gratitude was not short lived, either. On Boxing day that year, they arrived on my doorstep. Lucy was carrying a bag containing a huge bottle of falling down water for me, from her, for Christmas.

DIARY OF A DOTTY DOG DOCTOR

Comment:

On this occasion, the story had a happy ending, but I have been involved with many that didn't. Had Lucy's case actually been heard, she would now be dead, because she was out of control in a public place and she did cause an aggravated injury. The only thing her death would have proved is that the law really is an ass.

IT'S MUCH SAFER TO TALK ABOUT IT.

I now spend much of my time lecturing to various groups on the subject of behaviour. Most of these talks are serious, but occasionally, I get asked to do an evening talk for a club or society which is a much less formal affair. I enjoy talking anyway, but I especially like these evenings because although the audience is interested in the subject, they are primarily there to have some fun. Although it is me who is being paid to provide the fun, it is usually the audience who provide the most, or at least give me the opportunity of turning their comments into something that everyone finds amusing.

A classic example of this was when I was answering a question about coprophagia. This is the disgusting, but perfectly normal, canine behaviour of eating excrement - usually their own, but occasionally that of other dogs' as well. Some breeds are more prone to it than others; Labradors for example, are notorious stool eaters. It is mainly seen in puppies and they usually grow out of the habit but sometimes it persists into adulthood. One lady in the audience suddenly and almost proudly announced that she had a kennel of 15 Yorkshire Terriers and they were all coprophagic. Her question was how could she stop them. My suggestion was that she should not stop them, because it was cheaper to allow the habit to continue. Obviously, she wanted to know my reasons for saying this.

"It's common sense," I replied. "You only have to feed one of them."

Some people however, take things far too seriously - like the time when I told the audience that in my opinion, Border Collies must be stupid. I was relating the story of two dogs that I was watching in the local park, one was a Basset Hound and the other was a Border Collie and they were both running loose. The Basset owner called her dog, who, although looking up to show that the call had registered, totally ignored her and continued his hunting, shooting and fishing activities. The owner called again, with no response. She then started to perform all the stupid tricks that are designed to fool a dog, but don't. Running in the opposite direction, pretending to find something good to eat in her pocket, hiding behind trees and so on, but the Basset continued to enjoy himself. Occasionally, he would glance over to see what antics his owner was getting up to now, but I was sure that this was more like saying, 'keep shouting, I need to know where you are because you haven't got a collar on'. Then she tried to catch him, but whenever she got within a few yards of him, he just toddled off.

This whole performance lasted about 15 minutes and he eventually deigned to return to her, whereupon, he was told that he was a good boy - admittedly, through gritted teeth - but she had read somewhere that you should always praise your dog when it comes back to you. Obviously, the Basset had read the same book and knew he was on a winner.

The Collie, on the other hand was also having the time of his life, but as soon as the owner said "C..." the dog darted back - the owner never even had time to get the 'come' out. This dog was given a quick pat on the head, put on the lead and taken home a good 15 minutes before the Basset. All I asked the audience was, "Which one's the stupid dog?"
One of the women in the audience, immediately put her hand up and I thought she was going to answer the question as if it had been a serious one. With a face like thunder she stood up and blurted out,
"Have you ever trained a Border Collie?"
"Well yes, I have." I replied. "She was an explosive detection dog actually." This appeared to take the wind out of her sails, because she sat down immediately and never said another word. However, after the break, I

noticed that her seat was empty.

A couple of weeks later, a letter was published in one of the dog training magazines, which stated that the writer had attended a talk by a behaviourist, for whom she had always had a great deal of respect. However, all that respect had now gone because he said that Border Collies were stupid. The reason why she was so upset, the letter went on, was because she was an instructor at a training class and she worked Border Collies in obedience. Some of her students were at the talk and they would now say that her dogs were stupid. The letter did not mention my name, but hundreds of people who have attended any of my talks and read the letter would have known who she meant - I'm always saying that Border Collies are stupid. I decided that the whole thing was just too petty for words and chose not to respond. I didn't need to. The following edition's letters' page was full of people writing in my defence and the dog training fraternity well and truly put this woman in her place. They all got the point that I was trying to make, that from the dogs' point of view, instant obedience is less rewarding than total disobedience.

I actually don't think Border Collies are stupid. Any dog which spends all of its waking hours herding the goldfish in the patio pond, like my Border Collie did, can't be stupid - can it?

Often, some of the things people say can trigger me thinking about things in a whole new light. One example of this was during question time at the end of an evening talk. I had been concentrating on the modern way in which we live with our dogs, as opposed to how we used to live with them prior to central heating. In those days, heating was usually by coal fire and doors were kept closed to contain the heat. We also used to have a 'best room' which we only used when special visitors arrived, or at times like Christmas. This system of heating generally meant that dogs' freedom of movement was restricted and they would rarely be allowed into the best room, where the good furniture had to last a lifetime. Today, most homes have central heating and our environments are basically open plan, giving dogs more freedom of movement and access to all the rooms in the house. Added to this, we have become a much more affluent society and it is no longer an earth shattering disaster if the dog is caught sleeping on the sofa. The crux of my talk was that some dogs can take advantage of all this freedom and become so used to sitting on our furniture, or sleeping on our beds, that they will strongly object if we try to stop them. My conclusion was that if you don't want to create problems later, don't allow them the privileges to start with.

One lady in the audience asked a question about her problem dog. Her comments certainly seemed to suggest that many of the difficulties were indeed arising because of these privileges. She was adamant though that her dog knew the rules and was never allowed on their chairs or beds. I suggested that although he may not be allowed on them, perhaps he still attempted to get on them, or maybe used them in her absence.

"He certainly does not," came the confident reply. Then, in an equally confident manner she stated; "He has his own armchair and we let him have the bed in the spare bedroom and he only ever sleeps on that."

I was unable to give her a reply because of the noise being made by the audience laughing, which even the questioner joined in with, when she suddenly realised what she had said and what she had been doing. As I waited for the noise to die down a bit, I started to think more about this change in lifestyle and how lucky the modern dog is as a result of our more affluent lifestyle, compared with its forefathers of not that many years ago. I suddenly had a mental flashback of all the cars I had seen in the car park when I had arrived. In particular, the brand new Mercedes estate which I had parked alongside, with a sticker in the back window which read, 'Caution - Show Dogs in Transit'.

"I don't find it at all strange that someone would buy their dog a Parker reclining armchair and a four poster bed to sleep in," I said, as soon as I could resume talking.

"After all, I know that dog people are rich people." This caused quite a stir amongst the audience, with people scoffing at the idea that they should be thought of as rich.

"Do I take it that you are denying being rich?" I asked.

Clearly they were denying it.

"Well, take a look at all those cars in the car park." I said. "How many of them were bought for your dogs?"

There was a rising titter around the room as people realised that when they changed their cars, they had bought an estate model, or at least a car with the dog in mind.

"If you're not rich," I continued. "How many of you have moved house to one with a bigger garden and more room for the dog to play in?"

There was even more giggling and nodding going on as neighbour admitted to neighbour that yes, they had done that.

"So, you've bought your dog a new car, then you bought him a new house - you're starting to sound pretty rich to me. Tell me honestly," I continued. "How many of you have gone to the ultimate levels of financial extravagance and bought your dog a pet?"

There was a puzzled look on the faces of some members of the audience.

"How many of you bought another dog, so that your first dog would have someone to play with when you're out at work?"

That did it! They all erupted with laughter because most of them had two or more dogs. I was on safe ground saying this because it is fairly common amongst dog folk that when they consider getting another dog, they will justify their actions by commenting that it will be nice for Fido to have a friend to play with when they leave him at home.

"Now that's what I call rich!" I stated when the noise subsided again.

"That's nothing," said a man in the front row, "We're taking all our dogs on holiday next week."

I repeated his statement for those that were too far away to hear.

"I'm serious," he said in a voice that everyone could hear, "We're going abroad the week after and the dogs are going into kennels. We're giving them a week in the New Forest, so that they get a proper holiday as well."

"Well all I can say is, I rest my case," I replied. "Dog people are rich people."

"I always do that as well," said a woman from about halfway down the hall.

"Do what?" I asked, not quite sure where the voice had come from. She stood up and said, "Give my dogs a holiday of their own."

"I always buy mine a Christmas and birthday present," said a woman from somewhere off to the right of me. About half a dozen voices from various parts of the room all admitted to doing the same. Good God, I thought. This is getting like an AA meeting, they all want to confess to spending huge amounts of money on their dogs.

"And why shouldn't you," I said, almost as a way of absolving them from their sins of extravagance, "They are members of our family groups after all. I've been saving up to buy my dogs a bone," and I hurriedly changed the subject before they all started to shout out the things they had bought for their dogs.

Comment:
On the drive back home from this particular talk, it crossed my mind that all over the world there are people starving to death, yet we spend an absolute fortune on our dogs and some, it would seem, far more than others.

THE CASE OF THE MISSING BALLS

Dateline: November 1995

I have just received a phone call from a man, who came to see me with his wife and their dog - a two-year-old Old English Sheepdog - at the end of last year. The dog was showing aggression to other male dogs, but was overtly friendly with females (if you know what I mean). He was also overtly friendly with people's legs, cushions and anything he could wrap his front legs around, to stop them escaping from his amorous attentions.

The age of the onset of his aggressive behaviour, the fact that it was only directed towards males, his mounting behaviour and the realisation that he measured his walks, not in miles, but in telegraph poles, all pointed to the male hormone, testosterone, as being a key player in the problem.

"If you don't want to breed from him and as you don't show him, have you considered having him neutered?" I asked.

I saw the man cross his legs and visibly wince, as if I had just taken a knife to him and I thought, I'm going to meet a bit of opposition here. I was right.

"It's not an option," he said.

"It's a sensible option," I replied. "Everything points to the fact that his hormone levels are supercharged and, providing we initiate some behaviour programmes alongside having him neutered, we should get good results."

"Why don't we just do these programmes, whatever they are?" he countered.

"Because they will have more effect if the hormone which fuels a competitive attitude is reduced," I explained.

"It's not an option," he repeated. "I didn't drive all this way to hear you tell me to cut his balls off."

Do I detect a slight degree of antagonism here? I thought. His wife was looking very sheepish and was obviously not going to enter into this male arena where the trophy on offer was a pair of testicles.

"Just tell her what the procedures are and I'll go wait in the car," he said before storming out of the office. Well! I thought, don't mince your words, I'll take that as a no!

"He's totally against castration," said his wife, stating the blindingly obvious.
"I didn't suggest that we had him done," I replied, thinking it might not be a bad idea, after all.
"But he knew you were going to say that, it's what the vet suggested and he knows you all stick together."

So, he thinks there is a conspiracy between vets and behaviourists to collect as many testicles as they can, I thought.
"I can only repeat that the behaviour therapy will be more effective if we ensure that the high octane fuel which drives the desire to win is not available," I replied. "I can only give advice, I cannot make people take it."
I felt sorry for her, she obviously agreed with me, but she was not going to cross her husband and, as someone else with obviously high testosterone levels once said; 'this person's not for turning'. It is interesting to note at this point, that female lawyers in the US have been recorded as having very high testosterone levels, compared with women in other occupations. Footballers also record higher levels than vicars and, even more interesting, football supporters of the winning side have higher levels than those on the losing side. Add ten pints of lager and we can begin to see why trouble arises - though why English supporters should have such a bad reputation puzzles me.

I gave her a lot of advice about how to deal with her dog on a daily basis, especially in view of the fact that her husband travelled abroad so much. It was so easy to affect the behaviour of a young male dog by relying on him for comfort and support when her husband was away. We also discussed techniques of how to handle him in the presence of other male dogs, but I stressed (in her husband's absence) that it would all be so much easier if his maleness was reduced. She paid the bill and I walked with her to the car park. Her husband was decidedly stand-off-ish towards me and behaved as if I had a pair of shears behind my back, just waiting for the opportunity to go, SNIP - now you're a nice man.

Having met this sort of opposition from the male gender before, I thought no more about it, until I received a phone call from the lady some weeks later. "That's it!" she said. "I'm having him done. He's fighting with every dog he meets and he's even trying to hump the cat."
"Has your husband changed his mind?" I asked.
"No, but he's in America for three weeks, so he won't know."
"But he's going to find out at some point," I said. "He's not going to be a happy chappy."
"If he's that proud of them," she replied, "I'll ask the vet to put them in a glass jar. If he kicks up a stink, I'll have them mounted in plastic and he can wear them round his bloody neck."
She sounded pretty determined and totally different to the very meek lady who I had met.

A few days later, I received another call to say that her dog had been castrated. She also told me that as one of her friends was a vet nurse in the practice, she was in possession of the disputed parts of her dog's anatomy and had hidden them in a cupboard. I really didn't want to be involved with this, it was getting wackier by the minute - I mean, who does that sort of thing? Before the conversation finished, she added, "I don't think he'll notice they've gone anyway."

"Oh no, dogs are not like people," I replied. "He'll be bouncing around again in 24 hours."

"I didn't mean the dog, I meant my husband and if he does notice, I'll tell him he's a pervert for looking."

Other than having an occasional mental glimpse of a pair of lonely testicles in a jar in some dark cupboard, I forgot the whole affair. About four months later, I received another phone call, this time from the man.

"I just thought I'd ring you to tell you how well our dog is doing," he said.

"I'm pleased to hear that," I replied, thinking how amazing it is just how quickly anti-castration people change their minds when they see the difference it makes to their dog.

"Yes," he continued. "And you would have had his nuts off him." There was a supercilious sneer in his voice and I really wanted to deflate his egotistical balloon. Instead, I muttered something like; "Well, we don't always get it quite right."

Really, I wanted to say - look in the cupboard DER brain!

Comment:

Neutering a male is a relatively simple procedure, which rarely makes a behaviour problem worse and generally improves the dog's whole outlook on life in a pet environment. Neutering a female on the other hand, is a far more serious operation and, in some cases of aggression, might make the problem worse. A bitch in season can create an inconvenience to the owners and it is noticeable that people generally have no hesitation in having their bitch spayed, but convincing them to have their male castrated is another matter. Funnily enough, it is usually the male members of the family who object and I often wonder whether the age-old bond between man and dog goes further than companionship. I have my own personal views on this, but the whole subject would make for a very interesting PhD thesis.

DOMINANT DOGS OR JUST YOBS?

As you will have already realised, although my job description is 'pet behaviour counsellor', I wear many different types of hat. Author, lecturer, expert witness and of course, extremely talented gundog trainer. It's a question of checking my diary in the morning to see which hat I should be wearing for that day and sometimes, I have to wear a journalist's hat. I am often commissioned to write articles for the popular pet press and I have included the following article, simply because it takes a new look at an old subject. The subject I was asked to write about was, 'WHY DOES MY DOG THINK HE'S THE BOSS' and my immediate thought was; I don't believe he does. I knew that the magazine wanted me to write something along the lines of the dog being a pack animal and that they should respect us as pack leader etc, etc, but I really don't believe that dogs look upon us as other dogs and therefore do not compete with us for status. This is what I wrote instead.

It's very trendy to compare wolf behaviour to dog behaviour and to work on the assumption that because the dog is descended from the wolf, it must think like a wolf. For decades, we have looked upon the dog as a pack animal, which must live within a social group where there is a clear-cut hierarchical structure. All the training books will tell you that in order to keep your dog under control, you must let him know you are the leader of the group, or the Alpha figure. Since dog training started to become a popular pastime - shortly after the first world war - gaining this high rank in the eyes of the dog was basically achieved through strength. If the dog stepped out of line, he was punished and it is to the credit of the dog that the majority of them allowed us to do this.

More recently, gaining Alpha status has been achieved through more psychological methods, but still based upon how adult wolves would behave in a pack. It is said that the Alpha wolf would precede others through narrow openings, so don't let your dog push through doorways in front of you. The Alpha wolf would get the richest pickings from the kill by eating first, so make sure you eat before feeding your dog. Allowing your dog on your furniture and into your bedroom is telling it that it can sleep wherever it pleases and that this is a privilege granted only to the Alpha wolf. The list goes on to include things like high vantage points - don't let your dog sit at the top of the stairs, he will think he is the Alpha. Don't play tug games with your dog unless you start them and you end up winning them, putting the tug toy out of the dog's reach - the Alpha wolf owns all possessions and wins all tests of strength, and so on.

Pick up any modern book about dog training and behaviour and all the rules are laid out for us to follow. The trouble is, some people follow these rules too rigidly and end up having no relationship with their dog because they have suspected every move the dog has made as being the act of a plotting terrorist. When their new puppy comes bouncing into the room, they rush to the text books to see what a dominant tail wag looks like. Just in case the puppy does have designs on the throne, they go and sit in his bed, just to show him that they can. I wonder what dogs really think of us? I bet the word weird would be somewhere in the description.

The purpose of all these physical and mental gymnastics is to try and establish a dominant/submissive relationship between us and our dogs, with us being the more dominant. This is all fine, if it is how you want to live with your dog, but I have news that is going to disappoint a lot of people who have striven to reach this Alpha status - it all means diddly squat to your dogs. The most recent research from both the UK and the USA tells us that although the dog definitely is descended from the wolf (the mitrochondrial DNA profiles are indisputable), they have descended from wolves which, as a result of some genetic shift, were arrested in a juvenile stage of development. Missing out all of the impressive scientific data to support this statement, the bottom line as far as we are concerned is that the motivation for displaying true dominant behaviour is missing in the domestic dog simply because juvenile wolves do not compete for pack status. If this is the case, then why do some of our dogs appear to behave as if they think they are the boss? I have looked at this in some detail and the question I asked was; if domestic dogs do not have the dominant drives of an adult wolf, then why do so many dogs, who have been labelled as 'dominant', respond so well when the owner starts to behave like an Alpha wolf? To answer this question, we have to look at the dogs who have not responded at all and it is when we do this, that we can begin to answer the question posed by the title of the article.

Looking back through literally hundreds of case notes on 'dominant' dogs and how they responded to treatment, a pattern of success and failure started to emerge. In general, bigger dogs tended to respond well, while smaller dogs were far more resistant to the establishment of (what we used to call) rank reduction programmes.

To test this theory, I initiated a small research project, which at the time of writing is still underway, but the results so far seem to be confirming my initial findings. It is my belief that you can walk into almost any pet dog home in the country and ask the owners questions like; does your dog push through doorways? Does it get on your furniture and beds? Does it eat before you do? Invariably the answer would be yes to every question. Your conclusion could be that they have a dominant dog, but the majority of owners would disagree. One can see how easy it is to work up a dominant profile for a dog, but my suggestion is that this is how dogs behave, simply because our modern open-plan lifestyle allows them to behave like this. They don't do it for any point-scoring purpose, they do it because they can and because the owners let them. If a dog is allowed to do something which it finds rewarding on a regular basis and the owners then decide to try and stop it, the dog might object and these are the dogs that are accused of having a 'boss-type' attitude.

In this respect, dogs are no different from children who are allowed to do as they please, when they please. Parents are then surprised when the child throws a temper tantrum when they try to stop him or her from doing what has become the norm. Not surprisingly, and much like cute manipulative children, little dogs manage to engineer more daily rewarding behaviours than big dogs, and they do it simply because they are little dogs and therefore they can. Let me give you an example.

We all know that our dogs can tell the time! If you usually feed your dogs at 5pm, they will tell you it is nearly 5pm at 4.30pm - right? Well my dogs get fed at 5pm and they know it's nearly 5pm at 10.30am. I have a three-year-old Weimaraner called Toby and a 14-year-old Jack Russell called Chip and they are both 'food seeking missiles'. My wife had just bought a new horse (called Bill), who is very greedy and also very nosy. She usually brings our horses in at around 4.30pm, which becomes a signal to the dogs that it is nearly time for them to be fed - a very rewarding highlight of the day. Bill would take a mouthful of food and then pop his head over the stable door to look around whilst he munched the food. Inevitably, bits of food would drop on the stable base and Toby immediately spotted this as a good scavengeable source. As I passed by the stables, I saw Toby clearing up Bill's dropped food, while the nosy Bill was stretching his neck over the stable door to investigate

Toby. His nose was about two inches from Toby's back and I could just see a potentially injurious situation between two animals who really did not know each other.

I commented on this to my wife and she agreed, so Toby got shut in our garden area which overlooks the stables. Because feeding horses precedes feeding dogs, he was pretty excited and started to bark a lot, fuelled no doubt by the amount of food that Bill was dropping and which Toby thought he could make use of. All this barking woke up my Jack Russell who came out of the house, walked across the garden, slid under the fence rail and started to clear up the food which Bill was dropping - simply because she is small enough to be able to do it. My wife did not attempt to move Chip because we know she is rock solid with horses and anyway, Bill could not reach that far down.

Let's take a look at what would happen to my two dogs if they had both been diagnosed as dominant and I had been advised to lay down some of the rules we discussed earlier. Let's take the rule that we should eat before our dogs as an example. As previously stated, my dogs are usually fed their main meal after the horses have been fed at around 5pm. They start to get quite excited when the see the horses being led in, but the excitement starts before this. I have a neighbour who commutes by helicopter and invariably, he lands just before the horses are brought in. When my dogs hear the helicopter, they start suggesting to my wife that she should get the horses in, which will then mean that they will get fed. Actually, it starts before the helicopter arrives. Another neighbour drives a Jeep with a particular engine tone. When my dogs hear the Jeep, they rush around the garden looking up in the sky for the helicopter. 'See! There's the helicopter! Quick! Get the horses in! Right! Let's get the food.' Each one of these signals creates excitement and it is then confirmed that they were right to get excited when the next signal in the chain arrives. If truth were known, it probably all starts with the postman in the morning, especially with Toby, because food is very important to him. Let's assume then that the Jeep's in the garage, the chopper's on the landing pad, the horses are in the stables and the dogs are in the kitchen watching the food going into their bowls. By this time, their expectations of reward would be very high, so what would happen if we followed the standard advice and put the food out of the dogs' reach and sat down to eat ourselves. My Weimaraner would be devastated. Watching us eat would be the signal he would normally expect to see after he had eaten and he would probably be wandering around the kitchen, trying to figure out whether he had just enjoyed his meal or not. In effect, this procedure would have a massive punishing effect on Toby. It is a scientific fact that the removal of an expected reward is functionally and physiologically the same as a punishment, and the greater the expected reward, the more punishing the effect.

On the other hand, my Jack Russell is not quite so food motivated, although she still looks forward to her meals. She would take one look at what was going on, shrug her shoulders as if to say 'Oh! dear, they've been reading one of those dog books again'. She would probably go out through our cat flap, pop next door, go in through their cat flap and then eat their cat's food, which she does on a regular basis. My neighbour told me recently that they have to buy extra cat food because Chip is such a regular visitor; yet another example of a little dog reward that would not be available to a big dog. When she reckoned we would have finished messing about, she would come home and be fed. This neatly illustrates the same 'Alpha' rule having opposite effects on two dogs in the same house. Similar effects are likely with other rules and, if we consider the following scenario, we can see that the establishment and relevancy of higher-ranking privileges is entirely dependent on the individual dog.

It's an early winter morning. It is the custom to let your dogs out into the garden to relieve themselves. There has been 12 inches of snow overnight and you're still in your dressing gown. Just as you go to open the door, you remember that you have been told that you should go through doorways first. "Stay, stay, stay! Sit! Get back!" You have a difficult task controlling the enthusiasm of your thick-coated, long-legged Malamute, who is desperate to get into the garden and roll in the snow. Eventually, you control him enough to put one foot out first - that should satisfy protocol, you think to yourself, as your dog spins you in a circle in his rush to get past you. All this noise has woken up your other dog, who wanders out of the bedroom to see what all the fuss is about. This dog is a short-legged, rather well-endowed entire male Dachshund, who takes one look at the depth of snow and a quick glance at the length of his legs. "Stay!" You command. 'That'll do for me,' says the Dachshund and immediately returns to bed.

It is obvious from these two examples that controlling so-called 'dominant' behaviour depends entirely upon whether the dog is eager to obtain the resource which you are trying to control, or whether it considers it to be of high value. If it does, it will argue the right to have it, especially if it has been used to having it on demand for a long period of time. These are the dogs which give you the impression they think they're the boss, but I'm not convinced they actually perceive life in those terms, anymore than a spoilt child thinks that he or she is higher ranking than their parents. If you have an opportunist type of dog, or an opportunist child for that matter, and you allow them to do whatever they please, then they will behave in a brattish manner.

Calling such behaviour 'dominance' is a mis-diagnosis and trying to cure it by pretending you are Alpha wolf is a hit and miss technique. We need to look at what is important to the dog throughout the course of a day and take control of these areas. In particular, we need to look at the size of the dog and understand that little dogs can engineer many more rewarding behaviours for themselves than big dogs can.

My Jack Russell would totally accept me going first through doorways, eating before her, sitting in her bed, not allowing her on mine and letting me win all the tug games in the world. In fact, all of the things that so-called 'dominant' wolves display. I've tried all of these things with her and it doesn't make a jot of difference to her very typical JR attitude - but if I crept out in the middle of the night and nailed up my neighbour's cat flap, I might start to hit where it hurts. Until someone can prove to me that the Alpha wolf controls all cat flaps, I will continue to reject the idea that dogs think they are the boss. I will continue to treat them as spoilt brats who need to learn that their privileges are under the owner's control and that these are privileges to be earned and not rights to be demanded.

DO AS YOU'RE TOLD SOLLY.

Dateline: May 1994

Although I quite often make fun of some breeds, I have to say that I like all dogs and most people. Occasionally though, a dog will arrive with a huge attitude problem and when this happens, you can guarantee that the owner will have one, too.

Solomon was a grossly overweight, two-year-old Bloodhound and his owner was an equally large American lady lawyer. If you recall what I said earlier about American lady lawyers and testosterone levels, well, this one was walking proof - she had testosterone dripping out of her ears. Clearly, she was used to getting her own way. She arrived 45 minutes late and made no attempt to apologise, in fact, quite the opposite. As she climbed out of an open top two-seater sports car, which obviously needed a shoehorn to get both of them into in the first place, she complained bitterly about the pot-holes in the unmade lane that leads to my premises.

"You should have warned me about the state of your road," she whined. "I hit one of those holes so hard that Solly banged his head on the windscreen. It's quite upset him."

How do you answer an opening gambit like that? I'm awfully sorry, but it wasn't there 45 minutes ago when you should have been driving down the road? Oh dear! I hope he's not brain damaged? In England we drive around holes in the road? I resisted all of these thoughts and said instead, "Hello, I'm John Fisher, it's nice to meet you." To my surprise she totally ignored my greeting, got her Bloodhound out of the car and announced,

"I'll just take Solly for a walk," and set off down the lane, leaving me standing in the car park, totally bemused by the woman's attitude.

She was gone for almost 15 minutes and by now we were an hour behind.

I showed them down to the office and as she seated herself in one chair, Solly seated himself in another. Now, I don't particularly mind dogs sitting on my office furniture, it is after all an environment designed for dogs with problem behaviour, but whenever they do, the owners either apologise, tell their dogs to get off and say he doesn't do it at home (sure he doesn't), or ask if I mind. She said nothing and I swear Solly gave me a condescending sneer which said, 'So! are you going to take issue with her about this?'

"I need to use your bathroom," she said. Not may I, do you mind if, could I possibly, but I am going to.

Two thoughts crossed my mind as I directed her to the bathroom. First, is this consultation ever going to get started and second, Solly is going to learn to be a floor dog in his owner's absence. I gave him my best sneer back and realised that I was beginning not to like the dog because of his owner.

As soon as she was out of sight, I walked over to Solly and, pointing to the floor, told him to get off the chair. He just stared at me. This is dumb insolence, I irrationally thought and grabbing him by the collar, I pulled him off the chair. Solly looked up at the ceiling and started to howl like only a Bloodhound can - and he wouldn't stop. He kept up the blood-curdling noise until she returned from the bathroom and, as she hurried into the office she said,

"Whatever is the matter Solly?" Then, turning to me. "That's his upset sound, I can always tell when he's sad."

"He must really love you," I replied. "He started that as soon as you were out of sight."

No sooner had I finished the sentence than Solly had climbed back into the chair and was giving me an 'up yours' look. OK, I thought, dog: 1 - Fisher: 0, but there's plenty of time to go yet.

Almost an hour and a quarter of what is usually a two hour appointment had elapsed before I finally found out what they had come about. First, I had to listen to a long history of Solomon's ancestry. The way she told it, he shouldn't have been sitting in a chair, he really should have been on a throne.

"The trouble is," she said. "He's so well bred, he refuses to do anything I tell him."

"And you put that down to his breeding?" I asked in a surprised manner.

"Well, yes," she replied in a rather haughty way, obviously annoyed that I should question her judgement. "I'm sure he thinks that I'm beneath him."

I banished the hideous vision that this comment conjured up from my mind and asked her if Solly had ever had any formal training.

"He went to two lessons at a training class," she replied. "But I don't think he liked it, there were a lot of crossbred dogs in the class."

I couldn't believe what I was hearing; she was suggesting that Solly objected to mixing with dogs of dubious parentage, whereas it was obvious that she was the dog snob.

"There really is no substitute for proper training," I replied. "It sounds as if that is all Solly needs."

"Well, that's why I'm here," she said.

"But didn't your vet tell you that I don't run training sessions?" I asked. "I concentrate on behaviour problems."

"Well this is a behaviour problem," she argued, "He won't do as he's told."

"Yes, but it's a behaviour problem that can be cured by proper training," I told her. "You know, sit, down, stay, heel, come, etc, and I don't do that sort of thing."

"Are you saying you can't do that sort of training?" she asked.

"Oh, no! I can do it," I replied. "It's just that I refer training problems to one of our counsellors who also runs remedial training classes." As I spoke, I noticed that Solly was looking at me and he seemed to be saying 'she's a lawyer you know and she's just about to stuff you.'

"Well if you can do it, let's do it. As long as I'm here, we may as well teach him something."

"I'm afraid I have another appointment in about half an hour," I replied, desperately trying to get out of marching up and down the paddock trying to teach two overweight couch potatoes to understand each other.

"Half an hour is plenty of time," she said. "He only has to learn one thing and that's to do as he's told."

Solly was right, she had stuffed me and I was going to have to teach her something, even if it was just that there is more to training a dog than teaching it to do as it's told.

We started off on the stable base and I was going to teach Solly a simple sit and stay. Simple was how I imagined it would be, but I had not taken the Solly factor into account. Solly thought the word sit was reserved for when you are around armchairs, or near a wall where you can tuck one leg under your body and lean on it. A free-standing, unsupported sit was an alien concept to him. I started by trying to guide him into the correct position by using food rewards as a lure.

"I don't want you to bribe him," said the lawyer.

"It's not a bribe," I replied. "Once he knows what he's got to do to get the food, it then becomes a reward to be earned for the biggest, fastest and smartest response and for nothing less. I'll explain each stage as we get to it. At the moment I'm just using it to manipulate him into position."

"I don't want you to bribe him," she repeated. "I want him to do things because he's been told to do them."

"But until he knows just what he's got to do and what the command means, he won't be able to obey," I argued.

"We'll teach him what it means by some other method," she said with a hint of sarcasm in her voice. "I don't want him to learn that people, other than myself, can give him food - it gives burglars an advantage."

The way Solly was dribbling at the prospect of the smallest dog biscuit which I was holding in my hand, he was going to be a push-over for a burglar armed with a sausage - regardless of what she tried to teach him about where food came from. As this thought crossed my mind, Solly sat - completely unaided by any form of support - a truly amazing balancing act. Despite her former protest, I popped him the biscuit.

"Stop doing that," she almost screamed. "I've conveyed my wishes to you and I expect them to be respected." She continued in a tone which was bordering on the hysterical.

"Sorry," I said. "Force of habit. I believe that dogs should work for a reasonable wage just like we do." But secretly I was thinking, oh, shut up you old trout. "How hard would you work for just a pat on the head?" I asked. (I'm fairly adept at the old sarcasm myself.)

"Dogs are dogs and people are people," she replied.

Incredible, I thought, what an unbelievably stupid statement. How can anyone compete against the trained legal mind which is capable of coming up with such mind-blowing trivia as this? I suppressed the flow of thought to my lips, but did register the fact that I was now in an argumentative state of mind. No, let me rephrase that - I was now in the mood for a fight!

"Look," I said. "You are paying for my advice which I am trying to give, but I can't make you accept that advice. If you object to the way I train dogs, I suggest you take Solly to someone else."

My wife had been working in the tack room throughout this whole exchange and told me later that she was finding it all very amusing - that is until she heard me start a sentence off with the word 'Look'. At that point she knew

I was losing my cool and that my counselling skills were rapidly slipping away. To my surprise, the lawyer did not respond and for a moment there was an uneasy silence. Then I noticed that Solly was continuing to remain balanced in a sit position.

"Good boy," I told him. "Stay." I started to walk just a couple of paces away from him.

"Do as you're told Solly," said the lawyer, which of course caused Solly to get up and walk towards her.

"No Solly, come here and sit," I told him as I gently coaxed him back to me with his lead. Solly easily went back into the sit position.

"Good boy, stay," I repeated and started to move away again.

"Do as you're told Solly," she said again and up got Solly.

This happened three times and eventually I said,

"If you stopped distracting him, he probably would do as he's told."

"I'm not distracting him," she replied. "I'm giving him a command to do what you tell him. I only want him to obey other people when I tell him to."

I heard a stifled giggle coming from the tack room and I had to admit that I was beginning to see the funny side of this whole scenario. Her last comment pushed me way out of my depth and I suddenly had a mental image of me laying on my back, waving my legs in the air in total submission.

At this point, the bell rang at the car park gate and I realised that my next clients were ten minutes early. I felt a warm glow towards them and thoughts of giving them a free consultation crossed my mind. I'm pleased to say that I resisted this last thought, but the fact that it sprang to mind highlights the relief I felt at their arrival. All I had to do was to extricate myself from this blob of a Bloodhound and his control-mad mistress.

She paid the full two-hour consultation fee and then asked when I wanted to see them again - for some proper lessons - she added. I explained to her again that I generally do not do lessons and so each visit would have to be charged at the full consultation rate.

"That's extortionate," she said.

"I'm afraid that is the going rate for my time," I replied. "I cannot really reduce it just because I'm not conducting a proper consultation, it wouldn't be cost effective."

I resisted the urge to add, 'so you think lawyers can charge - watch this.' She told me that she would think about it and let me know and I added some remark about hoping she did and that Solly had got a lot of potential. I said this because we were walking past my smirking wife at the time and I wanted her to know that I had regained my 'be nice to the clients head'. I never did hear from her again, although I shuddered every time the phone rang for the next few weeks.

Comment:

During my frequent court appearances as an expert witness, I have locked swords with many lawyers who have attempted to discredit my testimony. I don't have a problem with this, because I know they are only doing a job and there is nothing personal in their comments. I see these same lawyers before court sittings, during the lunch break and at the end of the day and they are perfectly normal people. The lady with Solly however, carried her 'court room' attitude around with her. Maybe she was just a one-off.

What worried me about the whole affair when I reflected back on it later, was how her attitude to me affected what I thought about the dog. Why should I want to kick him off my chair, when I tolerate other dogs sitting on them? More importantly, when he howled the place down, why did I think he was doing it to get me into trouble? Was I so intimidated by the woman that I felt her dog was a threat to me as well? In hindsight, Solly was a very calm and unassuming dog who I would probably have liked, had he been owned by someone else - Bloodhounds are usually great characters. Perhaps Solly's character had just been flattened by his larger-than-life owner - who can tell? I certainly didn't want to experience a repeat performance to try and find out. These reflections after the event have certainly helped me in the long term because I now analyse my feelings for a particular dog, relative to my feelings about the owners. As I have said before, I like all dogs and most people and it certainly is not right that dogs should be tarred by their owner's brush. After all, they don't have much of a say in who they have to live with.

TOBY'S TALE, or TOBY'S TAIL?

Dateline: June 1992

I have mentioned our Weimaraner, Toby, in an earlier chapter and what follows is a short diary of events which occurred as he grew up and proved to me that learning theory is OK from a text book point of view, but in dog training we should really ask the dog what they think about things.

It had been over two years since Oliver, my wife's last Weimaraner, had died. Liz had been very attached to Oliver and it had taken this amount of time to reach a point where she felt that she was ready for another, hence Toby. Although at the time of his birth breeders were still legally allowed to dock tails (it is now an operation which can only be performed by a veterinary surgeon) we particularly wanted our new puppy to keep his on. Oliver had been docked in the customary manner and I had this theory that when you dock a Weimaraner's tail, all their brains fall out - so Toby's was not docked. Sadly, the theory does not hold true - he hasn't got any brains either. We collected him from the breeder when he was seven weeks old and he spent the first night with us in a hotel, en-route to our home. We wanted to make sure he arrived home in the morning, so that he would have a whole day to get used to the routine and the other dogs - our Jack Russell, Chip and our Japanese Akita, Yoko. Having a full day allowed us to get him used to his new bed for ten to 15 minute periods on his own and being left alone in the kitchen, which is where we eventually wanted him to sleep. This was preferable to arriving late in the day and then expecting him to cope with a long period of over-night isolation. If possible, we preferred him not to sleep in our bedroom and, although many people advise just leaving puppies to howl, hoping they'll soon get used to it, I don't see the sense in allowing young pups to become over stressed in a new environment. Instead, little and often practise bedtimes can very quickly desensitise them to the fear and strangeness of being on their own. It worked well for us, and by the evening, Toby was happily going into his new bed and we were able to shut the kitchen door without him complaining. In this respect, day one of his training was a success, but he learnt something else on that first day which we didn't intend him to learn.

Because of the infamous unpredictability of the puppy bladder, we allowed Toby numerous visits to the garden so that he could relieve himself if he wanted to. Toby thought this was heaven and with around an acre of new grounds to explore, he set about doing so with relish.

We know that puppies inherit certain characteristics from their parents and clearly, both Toby's mother and father were landscape gardeners, because from the moment he set foot in the garden he started the mammoth task of re-designing it. First, he dug a moat around the pampas grass, then he started to create a sunken garden in the middle of the shingle drive. We could see that he had plans for a huge swimming pool in the middle of the lawn, but this was obviously going to be a long-term project, which he didn't mind putting on hold now and again in order to eat part of his special diet. Didn't I mention the special diet he was on? Flower heads (especially yellow ones), soil (preferably freshly dug), slugs, snails and shingle (the former presumably for protein and the latter presumably for roughage). I don't know who designed the diet, but he obviously enjoyed it. In fact, he was enjoying everything about his new hunting, shooting and fishing lifestyle - yes, he had already found the goldfish pond.

In the middle of all this activity, I opened the kitchen door and, clapping my hands to attract his attention, called out; "Toby come! Pup, pup, pup, pup."

Short sharp sounds have a hurrying effect on puppies.

Toby came bounding across the garden, occasionally tripping over his ears, which were flapping in all directions. (Weimaraner puppies seem to be born with adult-sized ears, which they gradually grow into.) He skidded to a halt on the quarry tile kitchen floor. I shut the door, told him in a squeaky, happy tone of voice that he was a good boy and patted him on the head - you see, I've read the dog training books, in fact I've written the dog training books. Toby took one look at the shut door and another look at me and I could almost see a big question mark appear over his head. The look he gave me kind of said, 'you won't catch me with that one again', and we didn't! The next time I called him in from one of his garden adventures, he laid down in the middle of the orchard, put his wrinkled face on his outstretched front legs, arranged his ears so that they billowed along the ground on each side of his head and said, 'Shan't!'

Seven weeks old and after only one visit to the garden, he learnt that obeying a recall command means that you stop having fun and get shut in the kitchen. For sure, some human makes funny noises and bangs you on the top of the head - big deal! Out in the garden is great fun, shut in the kitchen is boring and, when you look at this from the dog's perspective, they're not wrong.

It's not a question of disobedience; at seven weeks of age puppies are no more capable of being disobedient than a human baby is - it's a question of rewards and loss of rewards. Conscious of just how quickly Toby could learn exactly the opposite of what I was trying to teach him, the trusty chicken skin was brought out of the fridge, a piece wafted in front of his nose and he followed me back to the kitchen. The door was shut, he was told in a squeaky, happy voice what a good boy he was, given a pat on the head and a piece of chicken skin to eat and then the door was opened and he was allowed out into the garden again. This was repeated a few times on that day and then occasionally over the next few days and he never refused to come in again. What this incident taught me, was not so much how dogs learn, but just how quickly they can learn and that they are not always learning what you think they are. A couple of other incidents from his training diary will highlight what I am saying.

When Toby was about 11 weeks old, I was with him in the paddock waiting for him to relieve himself. It was raining quite steadily, the sky was black and there was obviously a thunderstorm in the offing. I have often wondered what the medical reason is for dogs not being able to urinate when it is raining. Perhaps a reader with a veterinary background will be able to explain this to me, because you only have to look at people exercising their dogs in the rain, to see that they have to wait for hours before they are able to rush back into the dry. Well this medical phenomenon was happening to Toby on this particular day. I was walking around the paddock with my collar up against the rain, telling him to 'hurry up'. Toby was just following me around, making no effort to squat. Suddenly, there was a tremendous clap of thunder and, at the same instant, the heavens opened and the rain came down like stair rods. Toby's ears gave a convincing impression of an Indian elephant and he did what all puppies of that age are programmed to do - he headed at 90 miles an hour for the safety of the den. I started to run in out of the rain, when it suddenly dawned on me what was happening from his point of view. Prior to the thunderclap, he was obviously in a slight state of anxiety. He would have detected the change in atmospheric pressure due to the imminent storm and noticed that for some strange reason, I was walking around like the hunch back of Notre-Dame. On top of this, he would have registered the touch of impatience in my voice which might also cause him some concern, so when God suddenly shouted at him from above, that would have been all too much - primed to survive, he headed for the den. What do you think he would have thought if his pack leader had overtaken him and got there first? It would have convinced him that he was right to be frightened, because I was obviously frightened too. Instead, I stopped myself and had to stand in the pouring rain until this curious little head, still wearing the elephant ears, peeped around the corner to see what I was doing. "Oh, hi!" I said. "There you are. I was beginning to feel lonely out here. Let's walk slowly back to the house and crack open the biscuit barrel."

That's where we were for the rest of the storm, sitting next to the biscuit barrel and sharing a chocolate bon bon every two or three claps of thunder. Whenever you are desensitising to a potentially fearful situation, dog biscuits suck - really yummy, human grade choccy biccies are the way to a dog's brain.

Toby is not frightened of thunderstorms, and I don't know whether he would have been if I had run all the way back to the house with him to get out of the rain. I do know that there is a phenomenon called 'flash bulb' or 'one instance' learning. I also know that it is not necessarily what you do that rewards a behaviour sufficiently for it to become learned - what happens as a result of what you did confirms and establishes the behaviour (more of this in the next chapter). Most dogs are wary or anxious the first time they experience a thunderstorm. If the whole family rush to the window to watch the pretty patterns the lightning makes, the anxious dog might think; 'PANIC! They're all trying to climb out of the window - I'm going to hide under the bed.' If we then try to reassure the frightened dog with lots of calming 'didums, ba ba, coo coo' words, it might be perceived by that dog as a reward for its fearful behaviour. We can't win really, all we can do is be aware of how impressionable the young brain is and make sure that we print the right messages on it. In this respect, raising a puppy is no different to raising a young child. If mum is afraid of spiders, you can bet the daughter will be also. Dad will pretend he isn't and therefore, so will the son. Both of them are probably petrified, but through example, they will learn to cope with more confidence. If this is getting a bit deep into learning psychology (which is definitely not what this book is about), the next incident should make canine learning crystal clear.

Both Liz and I work from home. Liz runs a boarding cattery and I run my practice headquarters from a converted and extended stable, next to the cattery. Our bungalow sits in the middle of our grounds, so that our gardens surround our living accommodation.

To separate our private lives from our business lives, we have a large car park to one side of the property, a large entrance gate with a bell by the side of it for our clients to announce their arrival and a concealed drive (to the far side of a number of outbuildings) which leads to the stables, my office and the cattery. Halfway along this drive is a small gate which leads to our private gardens, but which gives us easy back access to the stables, the paddock, my office and the cattery. During business hours this gate is kept shut, effectively cutting off our personal lives from our business commitments.

Until Toby was old enough to be left the freedom of the house without chewing anything, whenever he was not supervised, he was left in the kitchen. The kitchen door leads to the front of the property and the car park. When a client arrived and rang the bell, my other dogs would run around the house barking furiously and so Toby learnt to run around the kitchen barking furiously. We would invariably leave by the kitchen door, patting Toby on the head as we did and telling him what a good ferocious guard dog he was. Within no time at all, whenever the bell rang, he would bark at the kitchen door, which suited us fine because we live in a fairly isolated area and a barking dog is an ideal deterrent against would-be wrongdoers. When he was about five months of age and at that gangly stage of development (all legs and ears), I was on the paddock with him playing Frisbee, when somebody arrived unexpectedly and rang the bell. A puzzled look came over Toby's face and then a light bulb went on over his head. He ran across the paddock and down the drive. He stopped and looked at the people at the entrance gate some 20 yards in front of him, then he shot through the side gate, ran across the garden, through the open patio doors into the lounge, across the lounge into the kitchen and barked at the kitchen door - because that's what he had learned to do! Here we were, thinking he was learning to defend the property, when in reality, in true Pavlovian style, he was learning that when you hear the bell, you bark at the kitchen door and it seems to please the humans. Stupid, I know, but he is a Weimaraner, tail or no tail. The visitors said that they had never seen anything so funny in all their lives. When they rang the bell, this totally uncoordinated floppy dog came running down the drive towards them, stopped about halfway down and looked at them, twisting his head from side to side. Just as they were about to speak to him, he shot out of sight and then in the distance they could hear a muffled 'woof, woof, woof'.

Of course, I explained to him what he was supposed to do and he felt such a fool for getting it wrong. He gets it right now and is a very effective guard dog. These are just three of the many incidents which happened as Toby developed and which taught me to always ask the question: we know what we are trying to teach, but do we know what the dog is learning?

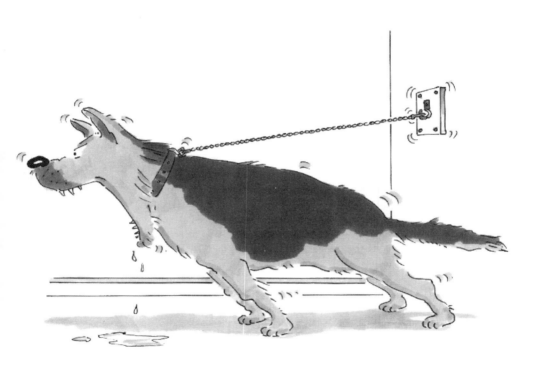

BEN'S TALE

Dateline: March 1996

Ben was a two-year-old German Shepherd Dog, well bred, well socialised well trained and owned by a very sensible couple called Jill and Dave. The problem with Ben was that he tried to bite people. Apparently up until around ten months of age, Ben had been very friendly and confident around people. In fact, the only thing Ben was frightened of was going to the vet's. As far as his owners knew, nothing untoward had happened to him on his previous visits and they were at a loss to know why he should be frightened. I explained to them that when some animals become fearful, they release fear pheromones which can be detected by their conspecifics (animals of the same species). It is the purpose of a pheromone to affect the behaviour of others and we know for example, when rats are placed in a box and given a mild electric shock, other rats who are subsequently placed in the same box instantly become frightened. It is highly probable that some dogs who are fearful at the vet's are not frightened because of any personal bad experience, but are merely reacting to the transmitted fears of others.

This might explain the reason why Ben trembled in the waiting room during a visit to check out a skin complaint. The nurse, who had known Ben since he was a puppy, recognised that he was frightened and approached him to give him a choc drop. Ben turned into the incredible hulk and lunged to the end of the lead snapping and snarling at her. Being an experienced veterinary nurse, she jumped backwards, and Jill, who was completely surprised by Ben's out-of-character behaviour, pulled him back and tried to gently calm him down. The vet heard the commotion and came into the waiting room to see what was happening. Seeing that Jill was having trouble trying to calm Ben down, he ushered them both into his consulting room and was able to examine Ben without a problem. At the end of the examination, he reached for a choc drop and leaned forward to offer it, telling Ben what a good boy he had been. Ben lunged again, this time even more aggressively. Being an experienced veterinary surgeon, he jumped back. Jill, now highly embarrassed by Ben's behaviour, tried to reassure him again, but Ben was having none of it, he wanted to kill the vet. Both of these incidents had happened within minutes of each other and it was the first time that Ben had shown any aggressive behaviour towards anyone or anything.

Two days later, Jill took Ben to the dog training club where they had been going since he was a puppy. As they stood waiting for the class to begin, one of the other students approached to speak to them.
Ben tried to attack the woman, but Jill managed to restrain him on the lead. The instructor saw what had happened and she approached to help calm Ben down. This time, Ben managed to bite and the instructor sustained quite a serious injury to her arm. There was no doubt about the intention of Ben's aggression. This was not a warning; four deep puncture wounds in apposition, clearly means that the dog intended to bite. From then on, Ben became aggressive to anyone approaching Jill, but only when he was restrained on a lead. He never did it when Dave had him on the lead and he was not aggressive towards people when he was off the lead with either Jill or Dave.

Of course, this led everyone to believe that Ben was defending Jill - the young male dog with his female owner syndrome - and Jill was told that she had to be more dominant over Ben. The more Jill tried, the worse Ben seemed to get and, as is not unusual in cases where 'dominance' advice is given, the relationship between Jill and Ben started to deteriorate as Jill tried to distance herself emotionally from him because the prospect of being forced into having him put to sleep was forever on the horizon. The dog club had told her that if he bit again, she would have no option other than to put him down, but they did offer to help her cure Ben's problem. They set up a situation where Ben was restrained on a lead by Jill and someone would approach them, holding a hand out to Ben. A choke chain was put around Ben's neck (Jill had always walked and trained Ben on a flat leather buckle collar) and instructions were given to adjust it so that it was high on his neck and sitting in the sockets just below his ears - a very vulnerable and very painful place to choke a dog. The moment he became aggressive, she was told to shout "NOOOO!" as loud as she could, take a pace back and yank as hard as she was able to, presumably to try and rearrange the shape of Ben's neck. The result of this medieval form of torture was that Ben's behaviour got worse. There is a lot of very sound scientific evidence to explain why this happened, which we will explore in more detail later.

Eventually, Ben's vet referred Jill and Dave to another behaviourist, who diagnosed Ben as being one of the most dangerous dogs he had seen and recommended euthanasia. According to Jill and Dave, the whole consultation was unpleasant, with cans full of pebbles being thrown at Ben and foul smelling substances being squirted at his nose every time he barked, which just resulted in Ben getting more and more angry as the process went on. The consultation ended with Jill sitting in the car in floods of tears, while Dave stayed a bit longer to express his feelings in no uncertain terms. Not surprisingly, the advice was rejected and Ben's owners insisted on a second opinion. This was how I came to be involved and after hearing the story about how the first few aggressive encounters occurred, was also the reason why Ben was tethered to a strong metal hook in my office. The hook was not there just to protect me, although it served this purpose admirably. The main reason why Ben was tethered was to show him that aggressive behaviour is just a complete waste of time. Before I explain how this works, we need to peek inside a laboratory and examine some experiments using dogs (but repeated with other mammalian species), which will help to explain why Ben was aggressive in the first place and give us a clue about how to cure it.

The relevant experiments involved teaching dogs to run down one side of a long corridor-like apparatus to the end where there was some food. The corridor was divided along its length into two equal sections by a low partition. Food was only ever available at the end of just one of these sections and so the dogs chose to remain in this half. Once it could be guaranteed that upon entering the apparatus the dogs would immediately run to the food end of the corridor, the experiment could begin. Just before they reached the food, a light was switched on, or a tone was sounded - which all the dogs ignored because it had no meaning to them. When they reached the food however, they received an electric shock causing them to escape, by jumping over the barrier to the other corridor where there was no shock and where they felt safe. After only one exposure, the dogs jumped to the safe side of the apparatus every time the warning light or tone was switched on and continued to do this for 200 trials. Before there is a public outcry demanding to know where this laboratory is and who is being cruel to dogs, let me explain that these experiments took place in the 1950s and were conducted to understand the effects of fear and stress in people - we are mammals, too. Hopefully, laboratory animals get a better deal today, but at least the experiments produced results which assist us in helping the Bens of this world. If you didn't like the idea of them receiving a shock after the first warning light or tone, then you're not going to be very impressed when you read what they did next.

As stated, the scientists were researching the effects of fear and stress and after 200 trials in which the dogs successfully avoided getting shocked, the point was raised that they can no longer be fearful or under any form of stress, simply because they knew how to cope after getting a warning.

The experimenters then decided to move the goal posts a little bit (well, actually they moved them quite a lot), and the new deal was as follows. If the light or tone is switched on and you go for the food, you won't get shocked. If you stand still, you won't get shocked, but if you jump to the other corridor, you will get shocked. The results that they achieved and were able to duplicate with other species, was that the majority of the dogs continued to jump to what had formerly been the 'safe side' of the apparatus. All of them showed clear signs of anxiety and most of them jumped quicker into the shock than they had when they were avoiding it.

Without turning this chapter into a scientific paper, the conclusions which can be drawn from this, and which directly relate to Ben's case, are as follows. Firstly, when the dogs avoided going near the food following the warning signal, the act of avoiding rewarded them. Secondly, the feeling of relief that they experienced when they jumped to the 'safe side' produced a secondary reward. In effect, what the dog does in a moment of fear or anxiety rewards the dog, what happens as a result of what it did produces a secondary reward which confirms and establishes the behaviour. Two rewards established the behaviour so successfully, that even when the researchers punished the behaviour, they could not extinguish it. In fact, the anxiety that this punishment caused resulted in the dogs jumping quicker. How does all this apply to Ben? Let's examine just what happened to him and relate it to the laboratory dogs.

Ben was at the vet's and he was in a highly anxious state of arousal. This means that his fight/flight system would have been primed and ready to fire if something happened which posed a threat to him. The nurse approached with her hand held out and Ben identified her as a threat (stupid, I know, but anxious states tend to cause over-reactions). What Ben did rewarded him, because the nurse beat a hasty retreat. What Jill did by pulling him away and trying to reassure him acted as the secondary reward. Because the same thing happened within five minutes and again two days later, the behaviour quickly became learned. Ben didn't need to be in a fearful or anxious state to show aggression under these circumstances, he had learned that when on a lead with Jill, if someone approaches lunge aggressively - it saves your life. There doesn't need to be a reason for it anymore, it's just what you do. Certainly, it wasn't a question of dominance, the only reason he didn't do it with Dave, is because he didn't learn it with Dave.

When the dog club and the behaviourist tried to punish the behaviour it got worse. Well, it would wouldn't it? Remember what happened to the laboratory dogs when they received a shock on the 'safe side' - they continued to jump into shock for 100 trials before the researchers gave up. All of them showed clear signs of anxiety and most of them jumped quicker. This in itself is a powerful argument against using punishment in dog training, yet it is still human nature to resort to punishment as a first technique to correct unwanted behaviour. What happens when punishment doesn't work? Well, we try something else. I wonder when we are ever going to learn to try something else first. With Ben tethered to my hook in the wall, something else was just what we were going to try, but before I tell you what that was, let me answer a burning question which is no doubt in your mind.

What should Jill have done instead of pulling Ben back? The training answer is nothing. She should have totally ignored what Ben had done, but in reality, she did exactly what you or I would have done under the circumstances.

Taken completely by surprise and totally out of character for Ben, all of us would have done just the same; it is only in hindsight that we can offer alternatives. For sure, Jill was no longer reassuring Ben, in fact she was now getting jolly cross with him, but she was still responding - and therefore continuing to be part of the process. If two rewards were involved in the learning of the behaviour, then we needed to identify these rewards and remove both of them. Here's how we did it.

Jill was sat on a two-seater cane settee right next to where Ben was tethered, so to all intents and purposes, he was on a lead next to Jill. In fact, he was on my lead and wearing a leather collar which I had supplied - when dealing with aggressive dogs, I need to trust the equipment. I briefed Jill on exactly what was going to happen and made sure she knew exactly what she should do before we started. I was going to wander into Ben's space - but not approach him head on with my hand held out. What I was looking for was the lowest level of arousal and if that was just suspicion, with slightly raised hackles or a low growl, then that's the level we were going to work at. It is pointless trying to work with a dog whose arousal levels have gone to the extreme, it's just not going to be open to any reasonable argument. I knew how long the lead was, I knew how strong the lead was, I knew how strong the collar and the hook on the wall was, therefore, as soon as Ben reacted, I was going to stand perfectly still.

Jill's involvement was to turn her back to him at the first sign of arousal and to remain in this position until I sat down again. When she returned to sit alongside him, she was not to touch him or talk to him and certainly not to praise him in any way. I explained to her that when a dog does something we don't want it to do and we stop it, or it stops itself, we usually tell it that it's a good dog. It's not a good dog, it shouldn't have done it in the first place, so we should not reward it for stopping (unless it's a puppy and just starting to learn about the rules). Having made sure she understood all of this, the procedure started.

I stood up and wandered over towards Ben, making sure that I avoided eye contact and keeping a slightly sideways profile, so that I didn't appear threatening in any way. Forget low level arousal! Ben got very angry, very quickly and even though I was expecting some form of aggression, it took a lot of self control not to flinch. At the same instant, Jill shuffled in her seat and exposed her back to Ben, but he didn't even notice, so intent was he on trying to get me to back off. I had told Jill that it didn't matter how long Ben ranted and raved, I would not go away until he calmed down. If Ben wanted to be aggressive, then that was going to be fine by me, my attitude was going to be - go ahead and do your worst, but you will find that it's not going to work anymore. The object of your aggression is not going to react and your mum is going to ignore you. As far as I was concerned, the fee for the consultation was going to be the same, even if Ben decided to spend the whole two hours trying to kill me.

Ben roared and lunged and snarled and spat at me for about four minutes, before he noticed that Jill was not looking. During this time, I just stood my ground, keeping up a constant low-level dialogue of complete gibberish. "Hi, Ben, how you doing? My! What big teeth you've got. Hey, what an impressive voice, ever thought about being an opera singer?" and so on. I made no attempt to get closer and I made no move to back away, I just stood there talking to the ground just in front of Ben's prancing feet and getting covered in spittle at the same time. I would defy anyone who has been involved with training dogs, or is just a pet dog owner, to allow this sort of behaviour to continue for so long without trying to stop it, or at least saying,

"For goodness sake, shut up!" However, the whole point of the exercise was to show Ben that he was on his own and failing to succeed.

As Ben got tired, he looked towards Jill - presumably to ask her to tell him to shut up, so that he could back out gracefully - the look on his face when he saw that she wasn't even looking was wonderful. At this point he alternated his aggressive shouting between me and Jill. Five angry barks in my direction and five towards Jill and he continued this for another minute or so. Then he reached a stage which I call 'popping down to the shops' It's almost as if the dog, realising that its current behaviour is not having the desired effect, looks at you as if to say, 'Look old boy, I'd love to spend the next ten minutes trying to eat you, but I was in the pet shop earlier and I think I've left my wallet on the counter.' When you see this look, you know that the dog is going to choose an alternative behaviour and in Ben's case, he pretended that he had spotted a mouse under the chair. This was my cue to walk away and when I sat down, Jill was able to turn round and sit next to Ben again - but with no verbal or physical contact.

After a few minutes, the procedure was repeated and Jill was warned that if she thought Ben was angry last time, through frustration, he would be even angrier this time. I was not wrong! I knew how strong the lead, collar and hook were, but I had not taken the strength of the wall into consideration, it bowed outwards as Ben went from lying down to absolutely ballistic as soon as I approached. Jill turned away again and I stood still and just waited. This time it only took about a minute before he noticed that Jill was not watching and as soon as he did, the tone of his barking changed instantly, but only towards Jill. German Shepherd Dogs are like no other breed in their ability to express their emotions vocally. Ben barked angrily at me and hysterically at Jill's back, angrily at me, hysterically at Jill - backwards and forwards for about another minute - then he spotted the mouse again.

On the third occasion, he threw about five barks at me, then he jumped on Jill's back, screaming hysterically and clawing her like crazy. I told her to just slide along the seat a bit, just out of his reach. "Thank you," she said without turning her head. Ben was obviously hurting her in his attempts to get her to respond. When he realised that he couldn't reach her, he went back to his mouse hunting. As I approached on the fourth occasion, he just looked at me and then looked under the chair. I told Jill to immediately make a big fuss of him and even help him to look for the mouse. Having chosen to display an alternative behaviour, Jill can now reward it, but the operative thing was that Ben chose the behaviour, he had not been told, or made to do it.

What he had learned on the three previous exposures, was that aggression does not get me to go away. Looking under the chair does, but with the added advantage of bringing Jill back, even if she did not speak to him. Now he could start to learn that looking away from anyone approaching also saves his life and that Jill would reward it every time. Of course, this one consultation did not cure Ben. Similar circumstances had to be set up with other people in different places, but the comment made by many people who have tried this technique is that once the dog starts to learn it, the whole thing snowballs at a very fast rate. We were fortunate that Ben's breeder was obviously interested in the outcome of our session and volunteered to arrange some 'two-reward' situations over the next few days.

Some time later, I was presenting a paper at the Royal Veterinary College on the two-reward theory of learning and I wanted to use Ben's case as an example. I suspected that the behaviourist who initially saw Ben might be in the audience and I contacted Jill and Dave to get the latest update on Ben's progress. According to Jill, he doesn't wear his heart on his sleeve like he used to, but at least he's alive and people are not at risk anymore. This was good news in one sense, but very sad in another. If people had only taken the time to understand why Ben behaved as he did in the first place, then he wouldn't have been exposed to all the punishment which only confirmed that the approach of people when he was with Jill was bad news. Although he is not lunging at people anymore, he obviously does not trust them and I can't say that I blame him for this.

As a final comment to this case, the audience at the RVC consisted of doctors, professors and men of letters from many different countries. I have noticed when talking to groups like this that they all like to categorise behavioural techniques with different titles. Counter conditioning, flooding, systematic desensitisation, instrumental conditioning and a whole host of other gobbledygook-type words. The more I thought about this technique, the more I realised that it didn't fall strictly under any one of these headings - it's a bit of this and a bit of that. With tongue in cheek, I told this august body that the technique was called 'instrumental counterfloosensitising' and I was amused to see many of them write it down. Although I haven't seen it used in any of the scientific literature on behaviour to date, I avidly scan the various journals to see whether I was successful in creating a new category.

WHEN I'M CALLING YOOOO!

Dateline: September 1995

I have always believed that education is vitally important, and that it shouldn't just be something that happens to other people. Learning, particularly about an animal as close to our hearts as the dog, should be accessible to all, and to that end I wrote and have tutored a correspondence course, called 'Understanding the Canine/Human Interface'. This course has been highly successful, with over 1,000 students having completed it from countries as far afield as India, Australia and the USA. Of course, one of the great advantages of a distance learning course is that the tutor never has to come in contact with the very little toads that we are talking about - the dogs, that is, and thus remains in possession of all his fingers while all about him are losing theirs. However, during a momentary lapse of concentration, I must have weakened and agreed to hold a teaching clinic for a local agricultural college which specialised in animal care courses for veterinary nurses and other students.

As if facing 40 real, live students all at once wasn't bad enough, I had somehow managed to allow myself to be talked into doing an actual practical behaviour consultation with them. No, not video presentations or a synopsis of a case which I had previously seen, and of course, solved, but a real case, brought in specially and totally unseen. Of course, this sort of trepidation adds greatly to the excitement of any kind of lecture, and the attendance numbers were the highest the college tutors had seen for a long time. It's amazing what the thought of a smallish behaviour counsellor being mauled by a largish dog can do for a previously jaded audience. Perhaps the students thought this was their one gambling opportunity of the term: at last the syllabus was about to be revitalised by a learning experience with a difference.

Having opened my talk with a brief discussion about behaviour problems in general, I welcomed the first 'case' of the day. Much to the disappointment of the slathering crowd, and to my great relief, in walked a delightful Springer Spaniel, followed by the young couple, Alan and Karen, who owned her. I made them as comfortable as is possible in front of 40 pairs of eyes, and we started the consultation.

The problem turned out to be a very common one. The owners reported that whenever they went out of the house, the dog would throw her head back and howl in the most grief-stricken and ear-splitting manner. Initially, their neighbours had been patient, and although they had told the couple that the dog was noisy during the mornings when both the owners were out at work, they had reassured them that they knew Shelby was only a puppy and would soon grow out of it. Now, however, the neighbours' tolerance was wearing thin, and they had reported Shelby to the local authority, saying if the couple couldn't resolve the problem, they would have to get rid of the dog. Shelby's owners were desperate - well, no one would opt to spend a morning in front of 40 teenagers conversing with a pet shrink by choice, would they?

Shelby, now 14 months old, had presented no other difficulties. As in so many cases, she was described as the 'perfect pet' - apart from this one problem! Gundogs generally are notorious for their desire to pick things up and hold them in their mouths. In fact, their obsession with objects is always in direct proportion to how much the owners don't want them to pick things up and hold them in their mouths. This is why the TV remote control is usually the dog's favourite chew toy, despite owning more dog toys than a pet shop. Shelby, however, was an exception. She had never really chewed anything much, and had never been destructive when left alone at home. She had also been house-trained easily and quickly. Shelby loved the car and was happy to settle quietly if left for a short while on the back seat.

Opening the discussion to the rest of the group, I invited any questions or suggestions as to what might be going on. The students asked lots of questions: always a blessing to a behaviour counsellor who needs to play for time while working on the diagnosis, treatment programme and likely outcome all in the space of four and a half minutes! Shelby was certainly attached to both her owners, and enjoyed attention and affection from them, but did not seem overly demanding. Her owners had always left her in the kitchen when they went out, and this seemed to be a reasonable routine. They had erected a child gate across the kitchen door, and put Shelby in there when they were about to leave, and also sometimes when Alan was working from home in his upstairs office.

Questions from the students kept coming in. Students asked about feeding regimes, medical ailments, ritualistic behavioural patterns and even the pitch of the howling. Everything seemed to be pointing towards a diagnosis of 'separation anxiety', where the dog simply cannot cope with being left alone at home without company. This is a relatively common scenario, and can often be accompanied by destructive behaviour, barking or even messing in the house. However, most dogs which do this usually show some form of over-dependence or over-attachment to their owners when they are with them in the house. This usually takes the form of the dog craving physical contact - having to touch their owner at all times - even when they are sitting on the loo or in the bath. Not a behaviour to be encouraged if you own a Great Dane.

Such 'clingy' dogs are usually fairly easy to spot - and so are their frazzled owners, who are usually desperate for a little privacy by the time they find their way to my practice. Dogs which suffer true separation anxiety may also show signs of anxiety when faced with novel situations - such as being stared at by 40 teenagers in the middle of a Wednesday morning. Shelby, on the other hand, strode round the room as if she owned the place. She tried valiantly to greet everyone at once, wagging her little stump of a tail frantically as she went. She was also the most outrageous little flirt - throwing herself on her back with her legs waving in the air at even the slightest hint of having her tummy tickled. This did not look like an anxious dog to me.

At this stage in a consultation, it is usual for me to ask the owners what they have already tried in order to solve the situation. As usual, they claimed to have tried everything. They had left the lights on in case she got scared in the dark, they left the radio playing to give her company and had littered the floor with newly bought dog toys, bones and chews. They had bought Shelby a new bed, and had put cosy blankets, and even some of their clothing into it, to act as a familiar smell. Alan and Karen had even discussed getting a pet for their pet, until they realised they might end up with two dogs howling when left, not only one.

Alan had even pretended to go out, and then peeked in through the window to see what Shelby was doing. Inexplicably, Shelby was reported as lying quietly asleep in the kitchen almost as soon as her owners were out of the door. She snoozed peacefully for a full 15 minutes, snoring gently and twitching in her sleep. Then, suddenly, she leapt to her feet, cocked her head on one side as if listening, threw her long Spaniel ears back, and howled. This session lasted about ten minutes, with a couple of breaks from her musical rendition to catch her breath in between.

In true 'call my bluff' style, the students were asked to make a formal diagnosis on the basis of the information they had heard so far - well, it's always advisable to let someone else get it wrong first! Cries of 'separation anxiety' echoed around the room. Suggestions of treatment ranged from teaching the dog to cope without her owners by cooling the bond between them, of leaving the house for practise separations and then coming back in unexpectedly, and even employing a house sitter.

Alan and Karen had listened intently to all the different suggestions offered. However, somewhere in the back of my mind the pieces just didn't add up. This was not a dog suffering separation anxiety, separation frustration or any kind of separation p......d off... something else just had to be maintaining the behaviour.

Then, in the best tradition of all good detective stories, a clue arrived bang on cue.

Alan innocently said, "A house-sitter wouldn't work. She does it even when we're there..."

A light went on somewhere in the old grey matter department.

"When you're actually in the house?"

"Yes," said Alan. "If I go upstairs to do some work I always leave Shelby in the kitchen. After about 15 minutes, she starts to howl."

"And what do you do about it?" I asked, intrigued.

"Well," Alan started. "I knock three times on the floor...." He paused, realising what he was saying, as he said it. "And she shuts up."

Blushing, and laughing at the same time, he said, "She's calling to see where I am, isn't she? And I've been replying. Talk about knock three times on the ceiling if you want me! I've trained her to do it, haven't I?"

I could almost see the light bulb come on over his head!

Comment:

Dogs are incredibly adaptable creatures. Their ability to learn about and manipulate new situations constantly amazes me. In my practice, we have a theory that dogs learn new behaviours after only four trials of performing a behaviour and getting rewarded for it. Of course, this means that, in theory anyway, training a dog to respond to basic requests such as sit and down is easy. It also means that for every one thing we are deliberately teaching our dogs, there are probably ten behaviours which we are inadvertently teaching them, too. Just think what your dog has learned in the time it's taken you to read this chapter. I'd go and put a padlock on the fridge door if I was you!

Dateline: October 1994

Every now and then, a new idea rears its head in the behaviour and training world. Such ideas range from the purely practical - car harnesses or head collars, which are useful, sensible and innovative, to the more 'unusual', such as sun hats or sanitary towels for dogs, which are not. However, just sometimes a truly unique and creative idea gives rise to new potentials within training or behaviour - and it is up to us to grasp it with both hands or reject it in favour of more conventional methods.

Clicker training is a fairly new concept in Britain. It has been an accepted idea in the States for some time, but like fast food and spin doctors, we took a little time to catch on across the pond. Clicker training originated in marine study programmes, and has been used to train all sorts of creatures, such as dolphins and killer whales, both for public 'shows' and to allow handling and control of such animals in captivity. Gentle training becomes essential when you consider having to give an injection to an adult male sea lion, or checking the teeth of a killer whale - where clearly the trainer cannot use compulsion to ensure compliance. The only way a killer whale will 'open wide' on command is if it wants to.

The clicker itself is a simple tool - more like a child's toy than a specialised piece of training equipment. Basically, when pressed, the tool makes a double-click sound, and this can be used as a signal to let the animal know it has performed correctly, and to expect a reward. In technical terms, such an association between the sound and, say, a piece of food, is a 'conditioned reinforcer' - in non-technical terms it is the equivalent of 'lights flashing, bell ringing' on a game show - it signals you got the question right and have won the jackpot!

The great advantage with such signals is that they are constant, and unvarying. Dog owners are usually told to, "Praise your dog!" by well-meaning instructors. This presents two problems. One is that human beings are not constant. "Good dog," uttered through gritted teeth after an hour of trying to recapture the beast in the park is simply not the same signal of reward as, "Good dog!" exclaimed by the owner who is celebrating a work promotion and has just enjoyed a pint or two down the local. The other difficulty is that killer whales do not relate particularly well to being told they are a "Good whale" while doing a mid-air back-flip - they need to know exactly and precisely what got them the bucket of fish at the end of it.

It's pretty important to stay one step ahead of new developments in the dog world, and I could see the potential in using such a neat signal in training straight away. However, the opportunities for practising it on unsuspecting dogs and owners seemed relatively limited. Those people with well-trained dogs seem strangely reluctant to allow training 'experiments' to be conducted on their pets, while those whose dogs have problems are usually far more interested in preventing it from biting them than playing around with clicking sounds. So, the question was, how was it possible to explore new and imaginative ways of using the clicker, not only as a training tool, but also as a possible tool in behaviour and attitude modification, without leaving a trail of practise cases behind me? Go abroad and practise there, of course!

This is not as calculating as it sounds. I had already lectured in Holland on several occasions, and had been warmly welcomed by the Dutch people. They had, in fact, been so enthusiastic about my visits that they had invited me back specially to hold an informal weekend of 'problem solving' and ad hoc training. What better platform for a journey into clicker-training? I arrived in Holland the evening before my lectures were due to start, and had a pleasant dinner with some of the delegates. Many of them had brought their dogs along, and were keen and willing to try new methods of training - in the interests of science, of course. It was also agreed that the lectures and training sessions would be filmed on video - always a useful, if somewhat nerve-wracking experience: the camera doesn't lie!

The following morning brought the delegates and dogs bright and early to the lecture hall. I talked for some time about various behavioural problems, and the potential use of clicker training in modifying behaviour which had not responded to other forms of treatment. In order to simplify the process of teaching, we decided to train some of the dogs to do very basic exercises. Having mastered this in no time at all, I asked if anyone had any more imaginative exercises or tricks they would like to teach. A young lady with a very cute Dutch Shepherd puppy volunteered. The dog was only about five months old, and looked much like the long-haired German Shepherd Dog that we're used to seeing here. Of course, the most distinguishing feature of nearly all puppies is that they seem to be born with adult-sized feet and ears - which the rest of the body grows to fit. This puppy's ears weren't only adult-sized; they were Jumbo-sized! Not only did the pup have ears to perform short flights with, mother Nature had somehow given them the ability to defy gravity - most of the time. Sometimes the dog's enormous ears stood up, while at other times they flopped down, exhausted.

This puppy was a bright spark. She already knew how to sit and lie down on command, as well as several other tricks, so we wanted something new and original to introduce her to the clicker. After some discussion, the owner decided we should try to shape the dog to turn its head in one direction. This would allow her to put the action on command, then extend it so that the dog would shake its head, as if disagreeing, on cue. I always have liked dogs that disagree with their owners.

'Shaping' means that the trainer waits for the animal to offer a behaviour which might, in any tiny way, resemble what they're looking for. First the clicker is sounded and the dog is given a tasty (little) food reward. This is to ensure that the dog won't startle at the sound and to condition him that it is a nice sound to hear. Once the sound is established as a signal of reward, we start to move the goal posts a bit. From now on, the dog has to train us to sound the signal - in effect, it has to do something to earn the click.

This meant that if Trudi, the puppy, turned her head even the smallest amount to the right, I would click, to mark the behaviour as being right, then give her a food treat. Of course, as soon as food is on offer, most dogs run through their full repertoire of previously learned behaviours to see what is going to win them the treat. Trudi started by doing a beautiful sit, then a down, then sat up again and gave me her paw. She sat quite still for about a minute, obviously in true Dutch Shepherd thought mode, then barked at me, twice loudly, then once no more than a throaty whisper. Confused, she turned to look to her owner for reassurance. Being an opportunist, I clicked and gave her the treat. We then went back to the beginning. Egged on by the reward of a food treat, but without a clue as to why she got it, Trudi went through her repertoire all over again, much to the delight of the watching audience.

After only about 30 seconds, Trudi again looked to her right, and received a click and treat. Then, she sat and looked at me. Obviously somewhat bemused, she looked over her right shoulder. Click and treat again.

We're on a winner here, I thought to myself, secretly smug that things were going so well so quickly. The next one will clinch it. Dogs often seem to learn new behaviours after four repetitions, and this one looked to be right on target. I waited. Nothing. I wiggled the food treat, just to let her know something was still on offer. Nothing. I waited some more. Nothing. By this time to say I was mildly surprised would be something of an understatement. Even when dogs don't know what you require, or are confused, they usually try to offer some behaviour. Trudi just sat there, doing nothing.

A hush had descended over the audience, as the spectators held their breath. To relax them a little, and to break any tension that the dog might be picking up, I suggested that we give Trudi a short 'time-out' period, just to get her back on track. She had a drink, and played with a toy. Without sounding too much like I was making excuses, I took the opportunity to explain to the group that animals are not machines - they don't necessarily perform to order, and they all learn at different rates. By the time she came back to the training session, I said, I was confident that she would be ready to make the next step.

Trudi came back refreshed and eager. She sat in front of me, gazing up, willing the food treat into her mouth. I waited. I wiggled the treat. Nothing. Then I asked her owner to shuffle about a little, just to encourage her to look round, so I could utilise the incidental behaviour. Trudi's head never moved. Her eyes flicked briefly to the right-hand side, but her head stayed riveted to the front. I clicked and treated. Sometimes we have to play with the only behaviours we are given, but this was not going to plan.

The audience were beginning to cough nervously. Mass embarrassment was starting to set in. Come on, puppy, I thought. Offer me something. Anything! Trudi sat, like a rock, staring at me unflinchingly.

I started to chat again, explaining that stress can sometimes inhibit behaviour. "Perhaps she's thinking I'm teaching her to sit still," I offered, pathetically. "Perhaps we'll have to reward even tinier pieces of behaviour before attempting to get her to turn her head. Maybe an eye flick to the right, or the smallest shift of her head. Maybe even an ear movement. Yes, perhaps I'll reward ear movements." Even as I said it, my brain was shifting gears. "Look at her ear!" offered someone from the audience, as I clicked and treated. Ripples of laughter were now coming from the front row. I clicked and treated again. Trudi's right ear was parallel with the ground, extended back as far as it would go. Her ear relaxed again. I took a chance and said, "Ear." It shot back and pinned itself behind her head. Her left ear remained fully upright, and her eyes never flickered. I clicked and treated. Even the back row could see what was going on now. This poor dog had been learning to stretch one ear as far back as it would possibly go, using all her little puppy strength and concentration, and I had been too busy looking for a head turn to even see it.

Within another two minutes, Trudi was almost turning her ear inside out on command to get the click and treat. To great applause, I handed her back to her owner, full of admiration for this little dog who had just taught me a wonderful lesson in about four minutes flat. Mind you, I had to have the last word. "You're going to find that really useful as you go through life!" I said. What better way to be upstaged than by a dog!

Comment:
Who's training who? Human beings are pretty arrogant when it comes to controlling animals, or even each other. This little puppy reminded me that no matter what we think we're trying to teach, dogs have a different view. Finding common ground is what good training is all about.

REAL DOGS DO EAT QUICHE

Dateline: August 1989

One of the few great penalties for doing a job which has so many rewards is that other people always believe my own dogs must be perfectly well behaved. This is a nice idea. I suppose teachers and driving instructors must have to put up with it, too, but the reality is, it's a little like saying that doctors' children must never get ill.

I have frequently been heard to claim that my dogs are never badly behaved - they are merely study cases! However, there have been one or two occasions where even I would admit that the two-footed side of the canine/human partnership has been pretty embarrassed at the behaviour of the four-footed half.

Of course, ask any parent when their child is most badly behaved and they will tell you - when it's most important for them not to be. This means that kids play up at serious family occasions, in front of the local vicar and, especially if attending any kind of function where a child psychologist happens to be present. So it is with dogs.

The year was 1989, and myself and three colleagues had set up a brand new organisation to try to ensure a quality and standard of behavioural counselling that veterinary surgeons and owners alike could rely on. In its early stages, the members of this new association needed to meet on a regular basis to discuss plans, and we had been holding these meetings at each others' houses, to minimise costs. Now it was my turn: the rest of the association were due to meet at my office for discussion, and then break for lunch.

Meeting over, four top canine behaviour specialists sat chatting in the garden, in the warmth of the summer sunshine. Of course, it should never be said that professional egos, particularly male ones, need bolstering, but put four men who claim to know a bit about dogs in one place, and the result is likely to be considerable amounts of bravado. Add one Jack Russell Terrier and the outcome is likely to be disastrous. For those that don't know about Jack Russells, I have some secrets in store. They are true terriers - feisty, determined and stubborn, but also charming, intelligent and incredibly cute. I used to say that most people are cured for life after owning one - but now I realise they are like an addiction for the masochistic - once you've had one, you just can't stop yourself from getting another. Chipper was our 'little personality'. At only about nine inches high she was a master trainer. She had taught the entire neighbourhood to take a different route to the common, rather than walk past her house, and she had given all the other local dogs a lesson in female Jack Russell law - what's mine's my own, and what's yours is mine, too, and don't you dare touch it. She had also taught me some incredible respect for dogs' speed of movement, restraint and determination. Most of all she taught me not to try to take her stick away from her when we went out for a walk!

Unfortunately, that day, there were those amongst us that had never been to Jack Russell training school - that's where the dog teaches the human how to behave - not the other way around. Indeed, even worse, present were those that thought they knew about training, and could 'cure' the little toad in five minutes where Fisher had failed for years. It started with one of them playing with a stick. He picked it up, and threw it. Chipper, for all the world looking like a normal dog, bounced after it, pounced on it, shook it a few times, and then lay down to chew it.

"What no retrieve?" One of my misguided colleagues was heard to exclaim.

With that, he got up and marched purposefully towards a very contented Jack Russell chewing sedately on the lawn.

"Come on, girl," he said. "Give us the stick."

Chipper went still, just for a spilt second, then went on chewing. He should have known he was beaten then. He should have returned to the fold where other equally defeated human beings sat, quietly disgruntled over ownership of a stick. But did he? That would be too easy! Thankfully, he had recognised the brief second of inactivity as being a terrier-type warning. Instead of reaching for the stick, which I feared he might, he bravely stepped forward and put his foot on the free end of the branch, leaving Chipper's jaws somewhere off the ground, clamped tightly around the other end. She was standing up now, determined not to let go, but also determined to reclaim the other end, too.

If you think this put her in a difficult position - you can imagine the dilemma of my colleague! Chipper had the upper hand. She started to inch her way along the stick, teeth getting closer and closer to the offending shoe by the second. Then, just at the point where stale-mate had occurred, the desire to keep the stick in her mouth was overcome by the annoyance of the situation. With a loud shout of triumph from my colleague, she let go. Unfortunately, his victory was short-lived. He may have had hold of the stick. Chipper had hold of his foot.

Lunch seemed just the thing to get over the embarrassment of the incident. My wife, Liz, who knows about these things, had decided that home catering could be a problem in our busy schedule, and that a little outside assistance needed to be called for. She therefore found a place which would supply 'home-cooked food without the hassle', just round the corner. Despite the rumour that real men don't eat it, this deli produced the most wonderful quiche - in both veggie and carnivore versions - to suit all tastes. Liz had collected the quiches, and had transported them home, a little rapidly, along our unmade-up road. Having got them into the kitchen, she was assessing the damage that road transport can do to a quiche, when barking started in the lane outside our house. Chipper - now fully recovered from her battle for stick supremacy - and obviously feeling somewhat inflated, had taken on a couple and their three black Labradors in the lane. They had not asked for rights of way, and were not going to get them. Liz dashed out to rescue the terrified dogs and their owners, apologising and cursing the delights of Jack Russell ownership at the same time. Having ushered the unrepentant Chipper back into the house, she returned to the kitchen to finish the preparations for lunch.

A hideous sight met her gaze. Quiche, boxes and pastry were littered across the floor. In the midst of the confusion stood Oliver, our large and very greedy Weimaraner, gulping down great mouthfuls of quiche as quickly as possible.

Resisting the urge to bellow as loudly as her lungs would allow, Liz gave in to admonishments of a quiet variety, before removing the smug Oliver from the kitchen and spending the next 15 minutes reforming what was left of the quiche into exotic shapes. With lunch now ready as it was ever going to be, myself and colleagues unwittingly sat down to a delicious meal of artistically arranged quiche and salad. Only one thing spoiled the meal. A rather subdued Oliver came and lay under the table as we were eating, but had to be put in the other room after several bouts of the most pungent flatulence imaginable. Unsurprisingly, Liz only ate salad.

Comment:

The motto of these and other misdeeds committed through the years by my own pets must surely be, 'do as I say, not do as I do'! Their antics may frequently be described as pets behaving badly, but they do provide wonderful opportunities for research and experimentation. Several books have been conceived and born through observations of my own dogs' behaviour. Indeed, perhaps 'Think Dog' should be re-titled 'Thank Dog' in their honour.

John Fisher 1947-1997

John Fisher, who inspired and enlightened a whole generation of owners, trainers and behaviourists, sadly died on 18th February 1997, prior to the publication of this book.

John's work with dogs and their owners spanned nearly three decades. He founded the Association of Pet Behaviour Counsellors in 1989, and took over the role of chairman from 1993 to 1995. John was also a director of the Centre of Applied Pet Ethology, and an international lecturer on all aspects of canine behaviour. In 1993 he set up and developed the Association of Pet Dog Trainers, in order to promote and teach kind, fair and effective methods of dog training in this country.

John wrote a correspondence course in canine behaviour which is administered by the Animal Care College. Recognised by the Department of Education as a vocational qualification, the course continues to attract students from as far away as Uganda, America and Australia. John's research into the development of behavioural and training aids resulted in products which are used successfully world-wide. He will probably be best remembered by thousands of owners and specialists by his books, Think Dog! Why Does My Dog? and Dogwise...The Natural Way to Train Your Dog which have become household names.

John is deeply missed by all who were privileged to know him. Many have lost a great friend and mentor, but the legacy of John's work will stand as a fitting and permanent memorial to a truly great man.

John will be remembered with love, laughter and the greatest respect by all those who knew him across the world.

This book stands as a tribute to John's work, his life and this 'Dotty Dog Doctor's' wonderful sense of humour.

Sarah Whitehead, Editor.